TEXTS and STUDIES

OF

THE JEWISH THEOLOGICAL SEMINARY
OF AMERICA

VOL. XIV

STUDIES IN DANIEL

THE STROOCK PUBLICATION FUND

*Established in Memory of Sol M. and Hilda W. Stroock and
Robert L. Stroock*

STUDIES IN DANIEL

by

H. LOUIS GINSBERG

SABATO MORAIS PROFESSOR OF BIBLE

The Jewish Theological Seminary of America

NEW YORK

THE JEWISH THEOLOGICAL SEMINARY OF AMERICA

5708–1948

PRINTED IN THE UNITED STATES OF AMERICA
PRESS OF THE JEWISH PUBLICATION SOCIETY
PHILADELPHIA, PENNA.

TABLE OF CONTENTS

FOREWORD xi

KEYS TO ABBREVIATIONS xiii

I Linguistic Notes on the Aramaic Portion 1

II Pre-Epiphanian and Epiphanian Four-Monarchy Theories 5

III The Writing on the Wall 24

IV On the Genesis of the Book 27

V The Hebrew of Daniel as a Translation 41

ADDENDA TO SECTION IV 62

NOTES 63

INDEX OF BIBLICAL AND RABBINIC PASSAGES 87

This is the second volume in the series published by the Stroock Fund in memory of Sol M. Stroock, Hilda Weil Stroock, and Robert Louis Stroock.

Sol M. Stroock was born in New York City in 1873. He was educated in the public schools, received his B.S. from the College of the City of New York in 1891 and his Master's Degree in Political Science from Columbia University a year later. In 1894, when he received his Law Degree from Columbia, he was awarded the Tappan Prize in Constitutional Law.

As a member of the Bar, he had an active and successful court and office practice. He was Chairman of the Committee on Character and Fitness of the Supreme Court of the State of New York for the First Department, from 1931 until his death, and he was associated with several important committees of the Bar Association of the City of New York and of the New York County Lawyers Association.

Mr. Stroock was associated with many educational institutions, including Columbia University, from which he received the Medal of Excellence in 1931 and where he was a member of the Board of Visitors of the Law School, and Harvard University where he was a member of the Committee to visit the Department of History of Harvard College.

Perhaps Sol M. Stroock's greatest interest in the educational field was in Jewish scholarship and research, an interest traditional among the Stroocks, of whom Professor Abraham Berliner, the historian, was a distinguished connection. Mr. Stroock was associated for many years with the Jewish Theological Seminary of America, which he served successively as President of the Executive Committee of the New York Branch from 1910 onward and Chairman of the Board of Directors from 1930 until his death. Together with his brothers he established at the Seminary the Abraham Berliner Prize in Jewish History in memory of their uncle. The income of the endowment is awarded biennially to the writer of the most significant work of research in Jewish history on a theme previously announced by the Faculty of the Seminary.

In recognition of his contributions to Jewish education, he received honorary doctorates in Hebrew Letters from the Jewish Institute of Religion in 1931 and the Jewish Theological Seminary in 1935.

In addition to his interests in learning, Mr. Stroock was connected with many philanthropic and social organizations. From 1926 to 1929 he was president of the Federation for the Support of Jewish Philanthropic Societies of New York and afterward served as Honorary Trustee at large. In 1924 he became a member and in 1934 chairman of the Executive Committee of the American Jewish Committee, an organization for the protection of civil and religious rights of Jews throughout the world. In 1941 he succeeded as president the late Dr. Cyrus Adler, with whom he had worked closely during many years of increasing crisis for the Jews of Europe. He served at various times as president of the Y. M. H. A. of New York and the Metropolitan League of Jewish Community Associations, as honorary director of Montefiore Hospital and as trustee and honorary secretary of Congregation B'nai Jeshurun. He was active in city as well as sectarian activities and a member of several organizations devoted to public welfare. In all these associations, Sol M. Stroock exhibited the same faith in the potentialities of the human being to reach ultimate fruition through learning and discipline. His intellectual and spiritual fervor combined with his practical insight into contemporary affairs made him an effective leader and a guide of unique value to the community of his day.

Hilda W. Stroock was associated with her husband in many of his varied interests, especially those primarily concerned with philanthropy. She was born in New York City in 1876, educated in the public schools, and graduated from Hunter College. She was particularly devoted to the welfare of children. One of her earliest interests was in the Montefiore Hospital for Chronic Diseases, where she later became Head of the Women's Auxiliary and then the first woman Trustee. She participated there in the founding of a Clinic for Cardiac Children, which she personally supervised for many years. She was responsible for the creation and management of the Mack Memorial summer camp for the benefit of the Cardiac Clinic children, and instrumental in adding much warmth to the lives of the patients, whom she always knew personally and to many of whom she remained for years a confidante and adviser. She was also active as Vice-President of the Westchester County Children's Association.

Mrs. Stroock was a woman of extraordinary energy, rare organizational skill, and great personal charm. She utilized her gifts not only in presiding over her home, in which her friends and her husband's gathered, but in supporting and leading the social causes which appealed to her. She shared her husband's interest in the Federation for the Support of Jewish Philanthropic Societies and in 1931 was Chairman of the Women's Division Emergency Appeal. In 1938 she was sponsor of the first Women's Conference on Jewish Affairs held at the Jewish Theological Seminary of America. She was a member of the Board of Directors of the State Conference of Social Work. In 1933, Mayor O'Brien appointed her to his City Work and Relief Administration, where she served as Vice-Chairman in the administering of all the relief work in the City.

ROBERT L. STROOCK, the elder son of Sol and Hilda Stroock, was born in 1905, educated at the Horace Mann School for Boys and received his B.A. in 1927 and his M.A. in 1928 from Harvard College.

He decided to make an interest in history the basis for his life work. Although he had always had a defective heart, he spent a rigorous year doing archaeology and research at the American School of Classical Studies in Athens in preparation for his Doctorate. During this period, he went on visits to Turkey, Egypt and Palestine. He was profoundly stimulated by his experiences and gave much consideration to the correlation of all historical and philosophical research. His letters written at the time and published after his death reflect his great thoughtfulness, his basic sense of himself as a scholar in the Jewish tradition, and the high ideals which he hoped to attain in the fields of learning and being.

He returned the following year to work again at Harvard, but fell ill of a disease connected with his heart and died in December 1930, after many months of suffering. Among his family, his friends and teachers he left a permanent void and a memory of one whose

> "* * * * * bloom, whose petals nipped before they blew
> "Died on the promise of the fruit * * * * * *"

A plaque in Robert Stroock's memory was placed in the halls of the Seminary by his parents. It depicts the great biblical characters, Hananiah, Mishael and Azariah, whose willingness to suffer martyrdom for their faith has been an inspiration for all generations.

FOREWORD

The book of Daniel, the earliest and most important monument of Jewish apocalyptic, is rather neglected both in and outside of academic circles. For the layman, the barriers to its enjoyment are well nigh insurmountable; and even the student of divinity or Semitics and his professor, after working through Daniel with a modern critical commentary, are apt to be left with a sense of frustration. They can not but feel that even modern scholarship is compelled to execute a number of exegetical tours de force and to posit a number of meaningless survivals of older traditions which can not be proved to have existed. Moreover, the book is partly in Aramaic and partly in Hebrew, and most of the Hebrew is wooden and artificial to a degree. The Hebrew text seems, on the whole, to allude to the events the pundits say it alludes to, but one may well wonder why it should do so in so ungrammatical, unidiomatic, and often unintelligible a manner.

The following five studies aim to make the book of Daniel more intelligible: to analyze it more finely than has been done before, and to determine the true purport and purpose of its component parts; to solve its unsolved major exegetical and literary problems; and to find satisfactory explanations for the more remarkable peculiarities of its languages. If they help readers to understand the book better, I shall be gratified. If they encourage investigators to give it more attention, I shall be delighted.

It is my pleasant duty to thank President Louis Finkelstein for including this volume in the series of Texts and Studies of The Jewish Theological Seminary of America, and the Jewish Publication Society for doing a fine job of printing.

The Index was prepared by my student Rabbi Gershon D. Cohen.

New York, June 1948.

H. L. G.

KEY TO BIBLIOGRAPHICAL ABBREVIATIONS

BAUMGARTNER *BD* = Walter Baumgartner, Das buch Daniel (= *Aus der welt der religion*: Alttestamentliche reihe, heft 1), Giessen 1926.

——— *BHK*[3] = *Biblia Hebraica*, editio tertia: Daniel (pp. 1255–1283) praeparavit W. Baumgartner, 1937.

——— *DF* = Walter Baumgartner, Ein vierteljahrhundert Danielforschung, *Theologishe rundschau*, neue folge, 11 (1939): 59–83, 125–144, 201–228.

BENTZEN = Aage Bentzen, *Daniel* (= Handbuch zum Alten Testament herausgegeben von Otto Eissfeldt: Erste reihe, 1).

BEVAN = A. A. Bevan, *A short commentary on the book of Daniel for the use of students*, Cambridge 1892.

B.-L. = H. Bauer und P. Leander, *Grammatik des Biblisch-Aramäischen*, 1927.

BICKERMAN *GM* = Elias Bickermann, *Der Gott der Makkabäer: untersuchungen über sinn und ursprung der makkabäischen erhebung*, Berlin 1937.

——— *IS* = Elias Bikerman, *Institutions des Séleucides*, Paris 1938.

——— *NHPC* = Elias J. Bickerman, Notes on Hellenistic and Parthian chronology, *Berytus* 8 (1944): 73–83.

CHARLES = R. H. Charles, *A critical and exegetical commentary on the book of Daniel; with introduction, indexes, and a new English translation*, Oxford 1929.

CIS = *Corpus inscriptionum Semiticarum.*

DRIVER = S. R. Driver, *The book of Daniel* (Cambridge Bible), 1900.

EISSFELDT = O. Eissfeldt, *Einleitung in das Alte Testament*, Tübingen 1934: 567–583.

HALLER = M. Haller, Das alter von Daniel 7, *Theologishe studien und kritiken* 93 (1920–21): 83–87.

HÖLSCHER = Gustav Hölscher, Die entstehung des buches Daniel, ibid. 92 (1919): 113–138.

KRAELING = Emil G. Kraeling, The handwriting on the wall, *Journal of biblical literature* 63 (1944): 11–18.

KKLK = H. L. Ginsberg, "King of kings" and "lord of kingdoms," *American journal of Semitic languages and literatures* 57 (1940): 71–74.

Montgomery = James A. Montgomery, *A critical and exegetical commentary on the book of Daniel* (International critical commentary), New York 1927.

Noth = Martin Noth, Zur komposition des buches Daniel, *Theologishe studien und kritiken*, 98–99 (1926): 143–163.

NSI = G. A. Cooke, *A text-book of North-Semitic inscriptions*, 1903.

Rowley *DM* = H. H. Rowley, *Darius the Mede and the four world empires in the book of Daniel*, 1935.

Sellin = Ernst Sellin, *Einleitung in das Alte Testament* (1st ed.) 1910: 129 f.; (5th ed.) 1929: 153 f.

Torrey 1909 = Charles Cutler Torrey, Notes on the Aramaic part of Daniel, reprinted from *Transactions of the Connecticut academy of arts and sciences*, vol. XV, July 1909: 241–282.

——— 1946 = Charles Cutler Torrey, Kings of the Medes and Persians, *Journal of the American Oriental Society* 66 (1946): 1–15.

Zimmermann 1938 = Frank Zimmermann, The Aramaic origin of Daniel 8–12, *Journal of biblical literature* 57 (1938): 258–272.

——— 1939 = Frank Zimmermann, Some verses in Daniel in the light of a translation hypothesis, ibid. 58 (1939): 349–354.

KEY TO SIGLA OF TEXTS AND VERSIONS

Lxx	= Septuagint
MT	= Masoretic text
Syr	= Syriac version or Peshitta
Th	= Theodotion
Vulg	= Vulgate

FURTHER LESS FAMILIAR ABBREVIATIONS

TB = Talmud Babylonicum　　TP = Talmud Palaestinense

I

LINGUISTIC NOTES ON THE ARAMAIC PORTION

A. A Second Grecism

A few years ago[1] I demonstrated that the phrase *mr' mlkyn* (Dan 2:47) is to be vocalized *mārē molḵīn* or *m. mulḵīn* and is an Aramaic rendering of *κύριος βασιλειῶν* 'lord of kingships,' the protocol of the Lagid kings of Egypt.

It is not the only translation-borrowing from the Greek that the book of Daniel contains. The Aramaic *'iddān* and its Hebrew translation[2] *mō'ēḏ* mean properly 'time, season,' but the former in 4:13, 20, 22, 29; 7:25 and the latter in 12:7 — not improbably in 11:29 too[3] — have the sense of 'year.' That this is purely an oracular affectation can not be plausibly maintained in the face of 4:22, 29. In the former verse Daniel is expounding to Nebuchadnezzar, who does not possess the gift of interpreting dreams, the purport of words heard by Nebuchadnezzar in a dream; yet instead of explaining that the phrase '7 *'iddānīn*' means '7 *šnīn* (years)' he merely repeats the former expression. It would therefore certainly seem that, so far as that expression was concerned, the angel 'had spoken in the language of men,' as the school of Rabbi Ishmael would have said. Again in v. 29, Nebuchadnezzar is not dreaming about an angel decreeing something about a tree but being told directly and literally, while wide awake, what is about to happen to him. Here too *šiḇ'ā 'iddānīn* would defeat its purpose if there were anything mysterious or ambiguous about it. A review of all the relevant passages suggests that *'iddān* has more or less the nuance of the French *année*, while *šnā* corresponds to the French *an*.

Now, we do not find *'iddān* (>*mō'ēḏ* in the Hebrew sections of Daniel) employed in the sense of 'year' outside the book of Daniel, but we do find χρόνος, properly 'time,' used in the sense of 'year' in Greek.[4] Ergo, Daniel's Aramaic *'iddān* 'year' is a Greek translation loanword, just like Koheleth's *taḥaṯ haššemeš* (ὑφ' ἡλίῳ) 'under heaven.'[5]

B. Two Morphological Observations

1. *The alleged Arabic-style passive haphel form in 7:4.*

The existence of forms like *hēṯāyū* (3:13), *hēṯāyiṯ* (6:18), *hu'al* (5:13), *hu'allū* (5:15), *hussaq* (6:24), *hūḇaḏ* (7:11) and *husᵃp̄aṯ* (4:33) by the side of *hᵒqīmaṯ* (7:4) is puzzling. Yet one hesitates to adapt the vocalizations of the first seven[5a] to the u . . . . i scheme of the latter because the former are so much more numerous, and feels prevented from adapting the latter to the former by the scriptio plena *hqymt*. However, a graph *hqmt* is available in v. 5, where it is passing strange; since the context there calls for the active *hᵉqīmaṯ*, as the Masoretes realized,[6] and the omission of a *y* to indicate a long *i* is suspicious in any post-Assyrian text. It will therefore be obvious, once it has been pointed out, that the spelling *hqymt* belongs in v. 5 and the spelling *hqmt* in v. 4, and that the latter is to be vocalized *hᵒqāmaṯ*. As a matter of fact, this form is represented in the masoretic *hᵒqīmaṯ*, which is nothing but a compromise between the passive *hᵒqāmaṯ* which the context requires and the active *hᵉqīmaṯ* which the received consonantal text offers. It is just as artificial as, for example, the vocalization *uṯp̄ōṣōṯīḵem* (Jer 25:34); which is a compromise between *uṯp̄ōṣōṯēḵem* 'and your scatterings,' which the consonantal spelling represents, and *wahp̄īṣōṯīḵem* 'and I will scatter you,' or better *wnippaṣtīḵem* 'and I will smash you,' which is required by the context. Or, without leaving Dan 7, we may observe that the abnormal vocalization *silqāṯ* in v. 8 is a compromise between the participle *sālqā* which would be normal after *wa'rū* (as after Heb. *whinnē*) in the narration of a dream (cf. vv. 2–3, 5, 6, 7; also 4:10, according to the masoretic pointing) and the perfect *silqaṯ* which the consonantal spelling represents. It follows that a genuine hophil does not exist in Aramaic.

Recent writers, to be sure, desiderate a passive form in v. 5 too,[7] and invoke the Versions, some manuscripts and editions of the original, and syntax. But the Versions only tell us how the translators understood the consonants, not how the author intended them to be understood; the Aramaic witnesses cited represent an obviously secondary text;[8] and the anomalous syntax of the majority of Aramaic manuscripts will have to be either accepted or remedied by changing something other than the verb. In defense of this syntax it might be argued that altho *śṭar* is a substantive in the absolute state, it may exceptionally have taken the accusative particle *l* for the sake of clarity, since it precedes the verb that governs it. However, I suspect that לשטר חד is to be emended to לשטרה חד 'one of its sides,' literally 'one its side'; cf. אחוכון חד 'one of your brothers,' literally 'one your brother,' in the Targums and Peshitta of Gen 42:19, 33. In such locutions, to be sure, the substantive may seem to us to be pretty indeterminate in meaning; but the pronominal suffix makes it determinate in form, and that may sometimes have availed it to attract a ל when governed directly by a transitive verb.

2. *The alleged loss of the feminine plural of the third person perfect.*

Disregarding the Neo-Syriac dialects, with their drastically revised morphology of the verb, we may say that from first to last the Aramaic dialects have preserved feminine plural forms distinct from the masculine not only in the imperfect but also in the perfect of the verb.[9] Only the Aramaic of Daniel seems to be an exception, which is very strange for such an early text. The grammarians are, of course, perfectly justified in refusing to believe that the ktibs *npqw* (5:5), *'t'qrw* (7:8), and *nplw* (7:20) are miswritten for the respective qre forms prescribed by the Masorah, seeing that the Hebrew ו bears no resemblance to the Hebrew ה or to the Hebrew א. However, the fem. pl. ending *ā* is purely Babylonian and targumic; whereas Christian and Samaritan Palestinian, as also — at least graphically — Syriac, use *ī*.[10] Since, therefore, the Aramaic text of Daniel swarms with waws that are miswritten for yods,[11] I for one can see no alternative to placing the final waws of our three verbal forms in the same category and reading *n̄páqī*, *'eṯ'qárī*, and *n̄pálī* respectively.

II

PRE-EPIPHANIAN AND EPIPHANIAN FOUR-MONARCHY THEORIES*

It was shown a few years ago[1] that the ultimate source of all four-monarchy theories is a three-monarchy doctrine of Achaemenian Persia, according to which the great Assyrian Empire (the founding of which was attributed to Ninus and Semiramis) had been inherited by the Medes and from them by the Persians. To this chain of three links Alexander the Great added a fourth, Macedonian, one when he absorbed the dominions of Darius III. However, the disgruntled non-Hellenic peoples of western Asia cherished a hope that the fourth would be followed by yet a fifth, native Oriental, monarchy.

Within the book of Daniel, as is well known, this theory of four monarchies and a fifth is represented twice; namely, in chapter 2 and in chapter 7. It is, however, in both cases modified in a characteristically Jewish manner both at the beginning and at the end. To the Jews, the absence of a Chaldean link from the succession of Empire-ruling kingdoms was incomprehensible. To them, in fact, the Chaldeans appeared to have a better claim than the Assyrians to be regarded as the Empire's founders; for the former had succeeded in absorbing the kingdom of Judah where the latter had failed.[2] Accordingly, both in Dan 2 and in Dan 7 the Chaldean monarchy has superseded the Assyrian; hence the absurd sequence Chaldean kingdom — Median kingdom (they were in reality contemporary successors to different parts of the Assyrian heritage) upon which the chronology of the whole book is predicated.[3] Again, we shall see directly that there were times when Jewry found Macedonian rule not intolerable as the reality of the present, but at no time could it possibly wax enthusiastic about yet a fifth heathen monarchy as the ideal of the future. The latter has therefore been eliminated from both Dan 2 and Dan 7.

But as is well known, they do not both present exactly the same thing in its room: or at least they do not both speak of it in the same way. Ch. 2 speaks in general terms of a fifth, worldwide and everlasting, empire to be set up by God (2:35b, 44); but it does not even hint at the Jewish nation's occupying a dominant position therein, let alone enlarge upon it. Ch. 7, on the other hand, is very specific to the effect that the annihilation of the fourth kingdom is to be followed by the bestowal of perpetual sovereignty over all the nations of the earth upon '(the people of) the holy ones of the Most High' (7:18, 27). This is only one of many divergences between the two four-kingdom apocalypses, basically similar tho they are. By itself, it might admit of many explanations, but it combines with the others to prove that *chapter 2 is pre-Epiphanian even in* — at least some[4] — *secondary elements,*[5] *and chapter 7 Epiphanian even in its primary stratum.*

Strange to say, one of the most valuable criteria for dating these chapters does not seem to have been applied before. Chapter 2 contemplates a survival of all of the first three kingdoms down to the moment when the fourth is liquidated. That is a natural inference from the dream, in which the upper parts of the statue only crumble to powder and fly away with the wind when the legs do (upon being struck by the stone cut out without hands, 2:34–35); and it is the only possible sense of one of the verses in the interpretation, which says that the kingdom of God will be established 'in the days of those kingdoms' (2:44).[6] Chapter 7, on the other hand, likewise suffers the second and the third kingdoms to linger on, after being shorn of imperial sway, until the moment arrives for 'the holy ones' to take over (7:12) — nay, it doubtless includes them among 'the dominions' (*šolṭānayyā*) that will acknowledge the latter's suzerainty but will, it seems, remain 'dominions' (see 7:27 end) — but it has the first monarchy destroyed long before.[7] It should be emphasized that only the 'son of man' (7:13) is identified with a people (7:18, 21, 22, 25, 27),[7a] whereas the parts of the image in ch. 2 and the beasts in ch. 7 are identified as *kingdoms*.[8] It is therefore the existence of a Babylonian, a Median, and a Persian *kingdom* that is presupposed by ch. 2, and the existence of a Median and a Persian, but of no Babylonian, *kingdom* that is presupposed by ch. 7. Scholars have not taken these survivals seriously,[9] but the texts manifestly do. And they have their reasons. There were actually *two* periods during the Greek age when the situation in this regard was that presupposed by ch. 2 and no fewer than *three* when it corresponded to the premises of ch. 7.

It is like this. Right thru the Greek age and well into the Roman, there existed residual Median and Persian kingdoms in the shape of the two more or less independent principalities of Atropatian Media,[10] called Atropatene for short, and Persis.[10a] In addition there was a Babylonian kingdom (1) from about 307 or 306, when Seleucus I adopted the title of king vis-à-vis his Oriental subjects,[10b] — and especially from 304, when he assumed it towards Hellenes as well, — until the battle of Ipsus, 301. For during this period Seleucus was confined to Babylonia and points east. (2) A Babylonian kingdom could again be said to exist (with two brief interruptions) during the three decades from 292 to 261. For from 292 to his death in 281 Seleucus I shared the royal title (βασιλεύς) with his successor Antiochus I, whom he placed in charge of his eastern dominions, and subsequently Antiochus I delegated the same authority in the same way first (279–268) to his son Seleucus and then (264–261) to a younger son, Antiochus II;[11] but after the latter became sole king in 261, there was no Babylonian kingdom in any sense. Now both these periods are pre-Epiphanian; ergo, ch. 2 is in any case pre-Epiphanian. The balance seems to me to be tipped in favor of the later of the two pre-Epiphanian periods by the Ptolemaic protocol 'lord of kingdoms' in v. 47.[12] It was evidently a current phrase with our writer, since he substitutes it for 'the Lord of lords' in a free rendering of Deut. 10:17, but is not known to have been assumed by any of the Diadochi but Ptolemy. That would seem to preclude the earlier of our two periods, during which Ptolemy at no time held both 'the Beautiful Land' (Dan 8:9; 11:16, 41) and the title of king. For the present, therefore, it is safer by far to identify the kingdom of Babylonia with one of the Seleucid co-regent crown-princes of 292–261,[13] and the 'divisions' of the Macedonian kingdom (2:41) with Ptolemy I or II and Seleucus I or (after 281) Antiochus I.[14] The Palestinian author will then be a subject of one of the first two Ptolemies: hence his familiarity with their title.

That ch. 2, apart from interpolations, was composed not later than the year 261 is confirmed by the fact that even some interpolated verses demonstrably date from the period 245–220 B.C.E., probably from near its beginning. The secondary elements in question are those words and phrases in the interpretation of Nebuchadnezzar's dream which introduce and expound features not included in the narration thereof, namely, the expression 'and the toes' in v. 41a and all of vv. 41b–43. These presuppose a situation where (1) the 'divisions' of the Macedonian monarchy have recently attempted a rapprochement by means of a matrimonial alliance, which, however, has ended in discord; and where (2) one division is exceedingly powerful and the other exceedingly feeble (v. 42). Close to four decades ago, Torrey[15] pointed out that these conditions are satisfied only by the period we have just named: 245–220 B.C.E. For it was only the first interdynastic marriage, that of Antiochus II with Berenice in 252, that ended in wrongs to the latter which her brother Ptolemy III avenged upon Antiochus II's successor (Seleucus II) by overrunning most of Syria and Babylonia in 246,[16] wresting some coastal areas permanently from Seleucid rule, and leaving it so weakened that Asia

Minor and the eastern satrapies shook it off until the rise of Antiochus III. The situation after the dynastic alliance of 197 was in no way analagous.[17] Torrey's only mistake was that he assigned the date which he had correctly determined for the words and phrases referred to above to the whole of ch. 2 — and indeed to the whole of Daniel A (=chs. 1–6) — whereas they are unquestionably later than the rest of ch. 2 (and the bulk of chs. 1–6), as we have pointed out. This accords perfectly with the limits 292–261 B.C.E. which we have already assigned to the body of ch. 2 on independent grounds.

As for the three periods during which only a Median and a Persian kingdom (i. e. Atropatene and Persis, as explained above), but no Babylonian, survived by the side of the now dominant Macedonian monarchy, they are those portions of the Greek age which lie respectively before, between, and after the two periods we have just considered; namely (1) ca. 330–ca. 305, (2) 300–292, and (3) 260–63 B.C.E. Time was, when practically all critical scholars would have agreed at once that only the last of these phases could be considered for the composition of Dan 7, for the simple reason that they were agreed that it was composed in the reign of Antiochus IV Epiphanes (175–163). However Sellin, in successive editions of his Introduction to the Old Testament, maintained that everything of Epiphanian date in the chapter was not merely (as others had maintained before him) ideologically but even literarily secondary; and in this he has been followed by leading critical Protestant writers on the Continent,[18] some of whom even date the original text in the lifetime of Alexander the Great (d. 323 B.C.E.), or early in the first of our three periods. I shall therefore proceed to prove the correctness of the older critical view.

There are first of all two considerations which create a general presumption in favor of a later dating for ch. 7 than for ch. 2: (1) its bitterness against the two most godless monarchies; (2) its less archaic symbolism.

(1) We have already noted that unlike ch. 2 it stresses the dominant role of the Jewish people in the kingdom of the future. Analogously, ch. 2 in no way implies that any of the four heathen monarchies are wicked, or that the termination of each one's dominance is the execution of a divine judgment based upon an examination of its record; whereas ch. 7 not only states this specifically (7:9–10)[19] but also, as we have seen, varies the sentences as follows: When the respective terms of ascendancy of the Chaldean and Macedonian kingdoms have expired, they are destroyed (7:4,11);[20] the Median and Persian kingdoms, on the other hand, are deprived of empire, but not of life (7:12). That the reason for the annihilation of the Macedonian kingdom is its brutality and godlessness is not only stated in the interpretation of the dream but implied by the description of the fourth beast (v. 7). That the original text of the description of the first and second beasts (vv. 4–5) implied that the first was likewise impious but the second had a redeeming spark of holiness will be proved further on. In short, the main point of ch. 2 is Daniel's cleverness (God-given, to be sure) in interpreting the dream of the Babylonian king, to whom it is positively cordial;[21] whereas the point of ch. 7 (in which Daniel plays a purely passive role, and has to have his own dreams interpreted to him by an angel) is God's justice — and it breathes hatred of the Babylonian and Macedonian kingdoms. Even Hölscher, who regards all clearly Epiphanian (or allegedly later) elements in the chapter as secondary, realizes that the marked anti-Greek bias of even indisputably primary verses indicates a later authorship than that of ch. 2.

(2) Again, in ch. 2 the four monarchies are represented by gold, silver, brass, and iron (in a later phase iron-and-tiling) respectively; but it is not the author's opinion that they themselves constitute a descending series, either spiritually or materially. For since, as we have already noted, he passes no moral judgments at all, we have no right to assume that he, any more than his colleague of

ch. 7 (or ch. 5!), could have rated Babylon, the desecrater of the Lord's temple, higher in the scale of morality than Media and Persia, which restored it; while in physical power he clearly regards the second, third, and fourth monarchies as an *ascending* series (2:39–40). His symbolism is therefore not allegorical but skeuomorphic. That is to say, originally — so still in Hesiod — the four-metal sequence represented the four ages of the world, which do constitute a descending series: but in our text the old vessel (Gr. *skeuos*) has been made to serve as a receptacle for, and as it were lent its shape (Gr. *morphē*) to, a new content; namely, the four empire-ruling monarchies, which do not constitute such a series intrinsically.[22] The symbolism of ch. 7, on the other hand, was a transparent allegory to everybody who shared its author's premises, as we shall set out in detail further on. And prima facie the version of the four-monarchy doctrine which carries over skeuomorphic, or vestigial, survivals of an older idea is likely to be more ancient than the one which uses only allegorical symbols invented ad hoc.

But we may go further and assert positively that ch. 7, even in its primary stratum, is a product of the reign of Antiochus IV Epiphanes (175–163) if we can establish that (1) vv. 7bβ, 20aα, and 24a with their 10 horns belong to the primary stratum; and (2) the tenth is Antiochus IV Epiphanes. So here goes.

(1) *Vv. 7bβ, 20aα, and 24a belong to the primary stratum.*

Sellin was right in assigning to a secondary stratum v. 8 — which (a) employs *'lū* where vv. 2, 5, 6, 7, and 13 have *'rū*,[23] (b) has perfects after it instead of participles,[23a] and (c) uses 'man' as a symbol of arrogance[23b] where vv. 4 and 13 use it as a symbol of holiness[24] — and with v. 8 all subsequent references to an eleventh horn. Tho he did not give a complete list of his excisions, he did specify *all* of vv. 20 and 24, so that he probably also regarded v. 7bβ, which equips the fourth beast with ten horns, as secondary; and this is done explicitly by all who have followed in his footsteps. But vv. 7bβ, 20aα, and 24a are all primary. Firstly, (a) because the situation in v. 24, in which the angel seems to say 'The 10 horns stand for 10 plus 1 kings,' can only be accounted for by the hypothesis that the 10 horns and 10 kings (v. 24a) are original, but the eleventh king (24b) has been grafted on by an interpolator who for once forgot to add an eleventh horn as well; secondly, (b) because the fourth beast must have a characteristic number if each of the others has, and that is demonstrably the case; and thirdly, (c) because the chapter is a torso without the aforementioned clauses, whereas it only gains in coherence by the elimination of all references to the eleventh horn — as we shall see. Of these three assertions, (a) requires no further comment; (b) and (c) we shall proceed to prove.

The characteristic number of the third beast (v. 6) is 4. That the number seems to be present twice would not in any case alter the fact that it is only one number; but as a matter of fact the 'four' in v. 6a is an intrusion from v. 6b. It was not the author's intention to number the wings, and he only had two in mind; for all he wanted to say in v. 6a was that the third beast was the next fiercest thing imaginable after the first (v. 4a). The first was like a lion (king of beasts) with the wings of an eagle (king of birds), and the third was like a leopard (one degree lower than the lion) with the wings of a bird (meaning no doubt one of the larger species, but not the eagle). The number of the eagle's wings of the first beast is not specified and therefore doubtless two, and the same is true of the bird's wings of the third in v. 6a as corrected.

As for the characteristic numbers of the first and the second beasts, (1) in our present text the former (v. 4) has none and the latter (v. 5) two: namely, 1 and 3. But this anomaly is only one of two *structural*, and several other, reasons why everything in v. 5 from 'and three' to the end must be transposed so as to follow directly on v. 4a. The other structural reason is this. (2) The fourth beast is represented as a second, more loathsome, edition of the first. We have already seen[25] that (a) only these two are annihilated. We may note further that (b) it is because the author has played out his trumps — for 'what is stronger than a lion?' (Jud 14:18; cf. 2 Sam 1:23b) — when he has likened thc first animal to a lion and an eagle that he can only say of the fourth that it was 'terrible, and dreadful, and strong exceedingly' and 'different from all the beasts that were before it.'[26] Consequently, when he states further that 'it had great teeth of iron <and claws of brass>'[27] it is obvious that it is not (as in our present text) to the second but to *the first* that he has previously ascribed 'three fangs[28] in its mouth [among its teeth]' (5aγ), and when he speaks of the fourth as 'devouring and crushing and trampling the rest with its feet' we know that it must have been again *the first* of which he related 'and it was commanded thus: Arise, eat much flesh.'

And here is a *zoological* argument. (3) Given both a bear and a lion, is it conceivable that a writer would stress the former's gluttonous consumption of meat to the exclusion of the latter's? especially an ancient Oriental writer; who did not know either the polar bear or the American grizzly, but only species that are omnivorous rather than carnivorous and attack large animals or human beings only when they are cross (e. g. a female when she has lost a cub,[29] 2 Sam 17:8; Hos 13:8; Prov 17:12)?

Or take the following *historiosophic* considerations. (4) It was the first kingdom that built up the Empire. But once the Empire existed another monarchy could take it over ready-made, as it were — perhaps even by invitation. That is precisely what the second monarchy — the Median, represented by Darius the Mede — is said to have done in Dan 6:1; 9:1. Moreover, Dan 2:37–39 says plainly that the Median monarchy is to be less grand than the Babylonian, and that only the Persian will (again) acquire dominion over the whole earth. The sequence 'eagle-lion, bear, bird-leopard' in ch. 7 is obviously intended to imply very much the same thing, and it can not have been its own author who obscured its implications by making the second beast out to be the most voracious of the three. Furthermore, since, as I have already mentioned,[30] our apocalyptists' notions of history are derived as much from prophecy as from history, it is pertinent to recall that gluttony (a metaphor for rapacity) as a national characteristic is otherwise predicated only of the Chaldeans; see Jer 5:15–17 (whatever may have been Jeremiah's intention, nobody in the second century B.C.E. doubted that 'the northern peril' of Jer 4–6 was the Chaldeans); Hab 2:5; cf. 1:14 ff. (the Chaldeans are named in 1:6). (5) That our author's notions of history required that the characteristic number of the first beast be 3 and that of the second beast 1 will become apparent when we have determined what these numbers stand for.

Meanwhile, this is the place to settle the question of the original location of the sentence 'It was set up on two feet like a man and given a man's heart,' whose incongruity at the end of v. 4 we have already noted. The answer is very simple: it belongs at the end of v. 5, in the position occupied in the present text by the words which we have just proved to have strayed thither from the middle of v. 4. Its present position is not only impossible for reasons of coherence[31] and — like the presence of 'and three fangs, etc.' in v. 5 (see above) — for reasons of historiosophy,[32] but also (again like the presence of the expressions just referred to in v. 5) disturbing from the point of view of natural history. For standing 'on feet like a man' in the sense of standing on the full length of the soles is never practiced by the lion but habitually by the bear (the parade example of a plantigrade), and in the sense of standing on the hind legs it is something the lion does rarely and the bear frequently; while 'a man's heart' is bestowed more naturally upon the more tamable animal. After 5aβ, on the other hand, the clauses that cause so much trouble in v. 4 are not only esthetically and zoologically unexceptionable, but eminently satisfactory historiosophically. Tho pagan ('a beast'), the Median kingdom is recognized to have had a spark of *holiness* ('human' qualities),[33] having been *consecrated* by the Lord (Isa 13:3, 17; cf. 21:2; Jer 51:28) to take vengeance of wicked Babylon for her *sacrilege* (Jer 51:11; cf. 50:28).[34] Observe, too, that the Medes, according to Isa 13:17–19, qualified for the beatitude of Ps 137:8–9.[35] Superfluous as it is, there is also a structural consideration of no little weight in favor of the transposition; namely, the parallelism to which we have already called attention between the first beast and the fourth. Both are ultra-'bestial,' both are destroyed, and — with 4bγ–δ restored to v. 5 — each is succeeded by a more 'human' figure: the less monstrous and less depraved Chaldean by the 'manlike' Mede, the indescribably hideous and satanic Macedonian by the godly 'son of man.'

Here, then, is a translation of Dan 7:1–7 with the foregoing transpositions and emendations:

> (1) In the first year of Belshazzar king of Babylon, Daniel had a dream and visions of his mind upon his couch: then he wrote the dream down and told the sum of the matters. (2) Daniel spake and said, I saw in my vision by night: behold, the four winds of heaven stirring up the great sea, (3) and four great beasts coming up from the sea, diverse one from another.[36] (4a) The first was like a lion with eagle's wings. (5aγ–b) It had three ⌜fangs⌝ in its mouth [among its teeth], and was commanded thus: Arise, eat much flesh. (4bα–β) As I looked on, its wings were plucked and it vanished from the earth. (5aα–β) And behold another, a second, beast resembling a bear, which raised one side.[37] (4bγ–δ) It was set up on feet like a man and given a man's heart. (6) After that I beheld and lo another, like a leopard with {four} bird's wings on its back. (This) beast had four heads, and was given dominion. (7) After that I beheld in visions of the night and lo a fourth beast, terrible, dreadful, and exceedingly powerful, with great iron teeth <and brazen claws>, devouring and crushing, and stamping the residue with its feet. It was different from all the beasts that were before it, and it had ten horns.

Surely, there can be no reasonable doubt but the ten horns of the fourth beast are every bit *as original* as the three fangs of the first, the one side of the second, and the four heads of the third. That they were in fact *more important* than the others to both the writer and his readers is evident from the sequel: it is only about their significance that Daniel inquires and is enlightened, yet nothing is missing.

To prove this, I shall now translate the balance of the chapter, distinguishing the expansions of the second apocalyptist by italics. If the reader will peruse the whole, omitting only the italicized matter, he will see for himself that (a) there are no lacunae and (b) the identity of the horns was from the beginning the most important thing in the chapter.

> (8) *I considered the horns; and behold, another horn, a little one,*[37a] *sprouted up among them, and three of the first horns were uprooted before it: and behold in this horn were eyes like the eyes of a man and a mouth speaking great things.* (9) As I looked on,
>
> thrones were placed,/
> and an Ancient of days did sit.[38]//
> His raiment looked like white snow,/
> the hair of his head like pure fleece.//[38a]
> His throne was fiery flames,/
> its wheels were blazing fire;//
> (10) A stream of fire went forth/
> and flowed from before it.//
> A thousand thousands ministered to him,/
> and a myriad of myriads stood before him.//
> The Tribunal[39] sat,/
> and books were opened.//
>
> (11) *I looked on.* Then[40] *because of the great words which the horn was speaking, as I looked on* the beast was slain and its body destroyed: it was committed to be burned by fire. [(12) As for the remaining beasts,[41] their dominion[42] had been taken[43]

away, but prolongation of life had been accorded them[43] until a time and a season.] (13) I saw in the visions of night:

Behold, with the clouds of the sky/
one in man's likeness was coming.//[44]
Arrived where the Ancient of days was,/
he was brought into his august presence.//
(14) To him was there given dominion — and glory
and kingship:/
all peoples, nations and tongues — him must they serve;//
his dominion to be everlasting — not passing away,/
never to perish his kingship.//

(15) As for me, Daniel, my spirit was troubled within me,[45] and the visions of my mind alarmed me.

(16) I went up to one of those standing by and asked him for the truth concerning all this; and, apprising me of the meaning of the matters, he said to me: (17) These great beasts, which are four, (signify that) four kingdoms[46] shall arise from the earth.

(18) But then saints[46a] of the Most High shall receive the kingship, and shall possess the kingship for ever, and for ever and ever. (19) Then I wished to learn the truth[47] about the fourth beast, which was different from all of them, exceedingly terrible, with teeth of iron and claws of brass, devouring, crushing, and stamping the residue with its feet, (20) and about the ten horns on its head *and another that had sprouted up and before which three had fallen; the said horn having eyes and a mouth speaking great things, and its stoutness*[47a] *surpassing that of its fellows.* [(21) *I saw that horn make war with saints*[48] *and prevail against them,* (22) *until the Ancient of days came, and the Tribunal <sat, and the dominion>*[48a] *was given to saints of the Most High*; *and when the time came, saints possessed the kingship.*]

(23) This is what he said: The fourth beast (signifies that) there shall be a fourth kingdom upon earth that shall be different from all the kingdoms, and shall devour the whole earth and trample it and crush it; (24) and the ten horns (signify that) from that kingdom there shall arise ten kings. *And another shall arise after them,*

and he shall be different from the first ones,/
and three kings shall he lay low.//

(25) *Yea, he shall utter words against the Most High,/ and saints of the Most High shall he harass,*[48b]
and shall think to change seasons and law; and they shall be delivered into his hand for a year, two years, and half a year.[49]
(26) But then the Tribunal shall sit, and its[50] dominion shall be taken away, to be destroyed and ended for all time. (27) And the kingship, dominion, and grandeur of all kingdoms under heaven shall be given to a people of saints of the Most High. Its kingship shall be an everlasting kingship, and all dominions shall serve and obey it. — (28) Here the matter ends. As for me, Daniel, my thoughts greatly alarmed me, so that my color changed. But I kept the matter in my heart.

No further proof is needed that the ten horns are original, that they stand for ten kings (v. 24a), and that consequently the numbered members of the first of three beasts also stand for kings. But Daniel neither asks nor is told about their numbers. The reason is obvious. The imperial power of the Babylonian, Median and Persian monarchies is a thing of the past, and for how many reigns each of them *did* exercise it is a question of purely historical interest. If the reader is bright enough to be able to identify the three fangs, the one side, and the four wings once the identity of the ten horns is revealed to him, well and good; if not, again well and good. For the burning question is: how long *will* the Macedonian kingdom remain supreme? This one is therefore answered directly: until the said kingdom has completed ten imperial reigns.[51]

(2) *The tenth horn is Antiochus Epiphanes.*

But the identification of the emperors of the fourth kingdom is, for us, less simple than that of the emperors of the first three, for two reasons: (a) There are more ways than one of counting Macedonian monarchs. (b) That the Macedonian kingdom would produce ten empire-rulers and no more was not an oracle after the event, but a genuine prediction not borne out by events; so that one can not find out whom the seer intended as the tenth by simply looking up who was the last. Let us, therefore, first prove that the other numbers stand for the supposed totals of the kings raised up by the first three kingdoms during their terms of dominance.

That this is the case with the four heads of the third beast has been surmised before, thanks to the circumstance that it is obvious from a comparison of Dan 11:2 with 10:1 that the fourth apocalypse (chs. 10–12) of Daniel B (chs. 7–12) also reckons with only four Persian kings. Why it does so has also been guessed. It is because Scripture furnished its author with only four names of Persian kings: Cyrus, Ahasuerus (=Xerxes), Artaxerxes, and 'Darius the Persian' (Neh 12:22). One recension of Seder 'olam zuṭṭa arrives at the identical result by the identical procedure;[52] and if rabbinic literature proper counts only three Persian sovereigns, that is because the Rabbis had a theory that the name 'Artaxerxes' was not distinctive but common to all Persian kings.[53]

By the same token, the one side raised by the second beast must represent the only Median emperor[54] known (from Daniel A) to our author: 'Darius the Mede.'[55] The Rabbis also count only this one Median prince.[56]

Did the author, then, assign three emperors to Babylonia? Of course he did. For if he determined their total by the same method as that of the Persian and Median superkings, that total was three, since the older books of the Bible (which of course included Daniel A) would have furnished him with the names of exactly three Chaldean emperors: Nebuchadnezzar, Evil-merodach (2 Ki 25:27 //Jer 52:31), and Belshazzar. Needless to say, therefore, the Rabbis[57] here too agree with the apocalyptist.[58]

But who are the ten Macedonian emperors?

According to Berossus, Antiochus I was the third king after Alexander the Great.[59] This counting disregards either Philip Arrhidaeus or Alexander Aegus; probably the former, since it was only the latter who lasted down to and beyond 312/11,[60] the year of Seleucus's assumption of power in Babylonia (and the one from which the Seleucid era takes its start).[61] According to Seleucid theory, then, the first ten Macedonian kings of Asia were: 1. Alexander I, 2. Alexander II, 3. Seleucus I, 4. Antiochus I, 5. Antiochus II, 6. Seleucus II, 7. Seleucus III, 8. Antiochus III, 9. Seleucus IV, 10. Antiochus IV (Epiphanes).[62] (Or, to put it in a form easy to remember: 2 Alexanders, 4 Seleuci, and 4 Antiochi.)

And surely, in no age but that of Antiochus Epiphanes (175–163) can the need have been felt for issuing a revised edition of ch. 2 — and who is so hardy as to deny even now that that is exactly what ch. 7 is? — for the purpose of specifying that (1) the fourth kingdom was the very incarnation of evil and (2) its destruction (at long last!) was imminent. It was precisely in response to the need — not felt in the happier days when ch. 2 was written — for an assurance on this last point that a new element was added to the numerology of ch. 2: — not only how many heathen *kingdoms* would successively attain world supremacy, but also how many *kings* from each kingdom would successively exercise it was predetermined; and Epiphanes was to be the very last emperor of the last heathen kingdom.

But who, then, is the little eleventh horn of the secondary stratum? To that question too the answer can only be: Antiochus Epiphanes. For neither the phrases printed in italics in our above translation of ch. 7 nor the verses which speak of the little horn in ch. 8 (viz., 8:9–14, 23–24) can have been written with anyone else in mind.[63] Now, these passages were obviously written after the desecration of the temple and the prohibition of Jewish religious observance late in the year 167 (but at the latest, before the king's amnesty in the winter of 164). Accordingly, the primary stratum of ch. 7 was in all probability written either prior to these measures or — barely possibly — immediately after, before months and years of life under the new conditions had brought their full import home.

That the nine years (especially the last year and a half) that preceded the crowning enormities of December 167 and the remainder of Antiochus's incumbency were calculated to fill earnest, self-respecting Jews with impatient longing for a deliverance from 'the bondage of the kingdoms' (*ši'būḏ malḵūyōṯ*), as the Rabbis call it, before the fourth kingdom produced another king[64] will surely be granted:[65] the core of Dan 7 is the voice of that yearning. Nor is it difficult to understand why after December 167 a bare indication that the fourth kingdom was wicked and would soon perish was no longer adequate, and unmistakable allusions to the specific iniquities of the tyrant who was 'diverse from the former' (7:24b) had to be added: this need was met by (chs. 8–12 and by) the interpolated clauses in Dan 7:

But three questions still remain to be answered.

1. How did the reviser come to count Epiphanes as the eleventh king, seeing that his predecessor had only a few years earlier — and correctly, as we have seen — counted him tenth?

2. Who are the three kings he says Epiphanes will humble (v. 24b)?

3. Who, according to him, are the seven other 'first horns' (v. 8)?

Various solutions are possible if one is not too fussy about plausibility and consistency.[66] But those who are, I venture to predict, will not remain satisfied permanently with any combination of answers but this:

1. The absence from the primary text of a clear allusion to Epiphanes' unexampled wickedness led the reviser to infer that that fiend was not included among the ten kings of the primary text. For Hölscher's observation (p. 120 below) that the expander has added to the original writer's discrimination between the last heathen *kingdom* and its predecessors (7bα, 19, 23) a discrimination between the last heathen *king* and his predecessors (20b, 24b) is absolutely sound.

2. Artaxias of Armenia and Ptolemies VI and VII of Egypt, all defeated by Antiochus Epiphanes.[67] As a matter of fact, Ptolemy VII had only been set up in opposition to his brother, Ptolemy VI, in 169 and then been reconciled with him. He therefore 'arose' later than Antiochus Epiphanes. But if the writer of v. 24b either did not know all the facts about Ptolemy VII, or chose to disregard this particular one, or adopted the fiction that *both* kings of Egypt had been reigning since the death of their father Ptolemy V in 181, the fault, if any, is the said writer's, not that of his exegete.

3. Seven other kings of western Asia and Greece: e. g., those of Pergamene, Cappadocia, Bithynia, Pontus, Commagene, Parthia, Sparta, Macedonia (Atropatian Media? Persis?). Pedantry is out of place here. It is quite probable that the reviser did not always pick the same seven himself. In fact he most likely treated the number 10 which he found in his *vorlage* as a round number just as — and just as erroneously as — Behrmann[67a] did after him.

In other words *the* reviser, or *second apocalyptist, of ch. 7 understood by the fourth beast* not the Seleucid kingdom but *the totality of the heathen kingdoms of his day* (at least of those within his purview). In this he was no doubt influenced to some extent by the analogy of the ram and the he-goat of ch. 8; each of which stands for a complex of *kingdoms* which are represented individually by its trunk horns, a king within a kingdom being represented only by a branch growing on a trunk.[68]

He may have excluded Atropatian Media and Persis out of deference to v. 12, which identifies them rather with the second and third beasts respectively, as we have seen. But if he could miss the bull's eye in his identification of the fourth beast, his identifications of the others may have been altogether wide of the mark; or he may not even have attempted any. The first apocalyptist had studied carefully both Daniel A and the other Scriptures bearing on the great powers to which the Jews had been subject since the loss of their kingdom: he therefore knew who the four kingdoms of Dan 2 were and was able to determine for himself the number of emperors each one had raised. The second apocalyptist, on the other hand, had studied primarily the texts which he supplemented. The texts, not the text. For in addition to Proto-chapter 7 he knew Proto-chapter 8 and Proto-chapters 10–12; and he expanded them all and wrote an independent apocalypse — ch. 9 — to boot, as will be shown in Section IV.

III

THE WRITING ON THE WALL

By now it is a commonplace[1] that (a) the words in Dan 5:25b are names of weights or (anachronistically) coins and (b) originally constituted a riddle, or metaphor, for a succession of personalities or regimes of varying calibers. But there is still no agreement (1) as to how many units are named, still less (2) as to what personalities or regimes they correspond to.

(1) In view of the overwhelming evidence of the Versions and Josephus,[2] and of the MT itself in vv. 26–27, there could be no real alternative to reading *mnē tqel pres*, meaning 'mina, shekel, half-mina,' in v. 25 unless the MT reading of the latter permitted of a vastly more probable solution.

(2) Kraeling[3] thinks it does. According to him, the MT of v. 25b, *mnē mnē tqel uparsīn*, means 'a mina, a mina, a shekel, and two half-minas' and answers the question: Of what quality were the kings after Nebuchadrezzar? The answer would imply that Evil-merodach (561–560) and Neriglissar (559–556) were quite great monarchs; 'the boy-king Labashi-Marduk, who was murdered after a reign of only 8 months in 556 B.C.E.,' was an insignificant one; and Nabonidus and the crownprince Belshazzar who sometimes deputized for him (but did *not* ever bear the royal title) were greater figures than Labashi-Marduk but still mere epigones. As a matter of fact, Kraeling is very close to the truth. But to quote him:[4] 'The riddle, or witticism, would have to have originated at a time when the actual events of Babylonian history were much better known than they were at the time of the author of the Aramaic part of Daniel ......' Moreover, it is strange that a source which even remembers the eight-month reign of the boy-

king Labashi-Marduk should already be under the delusion that Belshazzar was a king; nor is it clear why the list should begin with Neriglissar and not with the first Chaldean king, Nabopolassar, or at least with the great Nebuchadrezzar.

Actually, it does begin with Nebuchadrezzar; or rather Nebuchadnezzar, since the form with medial *r* was no longer in use in Aramaic at the time when it originated. For the reading with only three weights, in addition to being textually so much better attested, admits without any difficulty whatever of being interpreted as an epigram on the three Chaldean emperors known to the Jews of the Hellenistic and Roman ages: Nebuchadnezzar, Evil-merodach, and Belshazzar.[5] It was Nebuchadnezzar who conquered Judah: consequently he was, from the Jewish point of view, the founder not only of the neo-Babylonian empire but of *the* Empire;[6] see also Dan 2:37–38a; 4:19; 5:18–19. Belshazzar, who acquired it only by inheritance (and did not succeed in preserving it) obviously could not be placed on a par with Nebuchadnezzar. As for Evil-merodach, he had to his credit the release of Jehoiachin from prison (2 Ki 25:27–30//Jer 52:31–34), but apparently his name was against him. Its first element sounds merely sinister in English, but in Hebrew it sounds silly:[7] and while a wicked king can be great (witness Nebuchadnezzar), a foolish one can not. But of course, the circumstance that apart from his liberal treatment of Jehoiachin nothing was known about Evil-merodach (who as a matter of fact reigned only two years) but his name, whereas tradition had at least preserved some colorful legends (probably more than one) about Belshazzar, may have sufficed by itself to create the impression that the former was the least significant monarch of the three. In any case, 'mina, shekel, half-mina' means 'Nebuchadnezzar, Evil-merodach, Belshazzar.'

Now, upon reflection it strikes one that the conjectured sense implies one of the two things that the traditional one (Dan 5:26–27) emphasizes, namely that Belshazzar is to be the last of the Chaldean kings. What it lacks is the religious motivation of Dan 5:26–27. In other words, the relation of the later to what we have given reasons for assuming to have been the original solution of the mene-tekel riddle is very much like the relation of ch. 7 to ch. 2. The emphasis has been shifted from the cleverness of the interpreter to the justice of God: the three material weights have become a single spiritual weighing.[8] It is by no means a remote possibility that the more secular original solution also stood in a more secular context; that is to say, in a story in which Belshazzar did not behave sacrilegiously, or perhaps did not figure at all. For the solution would have sounded even more impressive in the reign of the *first* monarch of the series: try, for example, re-reading Dan 2:37–39, but substituting 'the mina' for 'the head of gold' at the end of v. 38, and 'like a half-mina' for 'of brass' in v. 39b.

IV

ON THE GENESIS OF THE BOOK

Section II has made it even clearer than it was before that there is a sharp break between Dan 1–6, or Daniel A, and Dan 7–12, or Daniel B.

A. Daniel A

To repeat what has been abundantly pointed out by Hölscher and others, Daniel A is a collection of six Oriental tales with a specifically Jewish interest (of which the first is mainly introductory) about successful courtiers. Daniel is the type of hero who rises high in royal favor by virtue of his uncanny gift of interpreting dreams and other portents ('the handwriting on the wall,' ch. 5).[1] Tho one of the dreams he interprets happens to predict the succession of pagan empires and the ultimate establishment of God's kingdom upon earth, the purpose of the story in question (ch. 2) is to stress not the imminence of this last event or even, primarily, its inevitability (tho it has that purpose too), but Daniel's amazing feat in reading four centuries of future world history and a breath-taking eschatology in the multi-metal colossus and the mysterious stone of Nebuchadnezzar's dream. Surely the major religious lesson of the story is that such wisdom can only be conferred by the true God (vv. 17–23, 27–28, 47). As for Nebuchadnezzar's behavior thru it all, the acuity of vision that is able to discern in it a satire upon Antiochus IV is not to be envied. Again, ch. 6 recalls irresistibly the stories of how the rivals of the courtiers Ahikar and Mordecai (in the book of Esther) plotted the destruction of these men but only brought about their own. But of course the

Jewish religious coloring is there. The *way* in which the jealous rivals try to get rid of Daniel and compass their own undoing is by luring the unsuspecting Darius the Mede (for a heathen a model prince, never a mere code-word for Antiochus Epiphanes!) into legislation to which most Jews would respond by abstaining from *all* worship for thirty days but which Daniel, they rightly anticipated, would openly flout. In a parallel tale, ch. 3, the religious interest has almost obliterated the original motif: those who denounce the three Jewish officials are not identical with the executioners who get executed, and altho the designation 'Chaldean men' (3:8) and the fact that they have direct access to the king imply that they were officials, it is possible to miss the motif of professional rivalry if one is not looking for it (but do look at v. 12a!). Here too, however, it should be noted that the royal whim created a problem of conscience only for the very few Jews whose approach within earshot of the orchestra in the plain of Dura was rendered unavoidable by some official business. It is a tale in which Palestinian Jews in the years 167–4 could doubtless find a timely message for themselves (as also in national petitions like Psalm 79, which a bygone era of biblical criticism naively identified as 'Maccabean'), but it can not have been written by people in their situation. It is the same in ch. 4. God humbles the proud. But Nebuchadnezzar's pride did not take the form of insisting that Daniel — whose reputation as an interpreter of dreams is once again brilliantly vindicated, as the heathen magicians, soothsayers, etc., once again miserably fail — should forsake the worship of his God and the practice of his religion. In ch. 5, finally, Belshazzar is punished for the shocking misuse of the vessels of the temple of Jerusalem in a sort of ritual banquet in honor of lifeless idols. Neither Daniel — whose exegetical genius once again puts all hermeneutic science to shame and is rewarded with very high office — nor any other Jew is obliged to participate in such impious conviviality or to eat unclean meats or profane sabbaths and festivals. Nor, be it noted, are Jews tempted to do anything of the sort by being given preference over Jews of Daniel's type.

Within Daniel A, apart from the small interpolations in ch. 2 and odd glosses, no *literary* stratification has, so far as I know, been demonstrated. (That the stories are shown by certain discrepancies to have been originally independent tales does not make them distinct *documents*. Neither are the earlier forms of the mene-tekel riddle and of the mene-tekel story that can be surmised from Dan 5 — see Section III — and similar reconstructions of older traditions, literary documents present in the book of Daniel.)

With all this the dating of ch. 2 which resulted from the first few pages of Section II — between 292 and 261 B.C.E. for the body, and between 246 and 220 B.C.E. for some two and a half secondary verses — agrees perfectly.

B. Daniel B

A totally different picture confronts us in Daniel B. Here we have no court tales but four apocalypses — chs. 7, 8, 9 and 10–12 — and every one of them bears the imprint of the reign of Antiochus IV.

Ch. 7, as we know already from Section II, consists of an original apocalypse, complete in itself, and a later strand that has been woven into it. Let us call the basic text of ch. 7 Ba and the added strand, since we printed it in italics in Section II, *Ba*; and for the present let us dispense with any special sigla for chs. 8–12 or any parts thereof. Ba, it will be recalled, is from the reign of Antiochus IV since it knows ten Macedonian monarchs; but while its unreserved condemnation of the fourth kingdom and its anticipation of its complete annihilation in the reign of its present king are no doubt reflexes of his commercial exploitation of the high priesthood of the Jerusalem temple, of his encouragement of the Hellenizers, probably of his looting of the temple in 169, and perhaps even of his 'abolition of the Jewish temple-state' and 'founding of a polis upon the Akra' in the summer of 168,'[2] the absence of any reference to a desecration of the temple or to a religious persecution of the Jews and of any specific denunciation of the tenth king of the fourth kingdom would hardly be conceivable if Ba knew of the desecration of the temple and the beginning of the religious persecution in or about December 167. The other three apocalypses, on the other hand, notoriously do refer to these events without exception (8:11–12, 24–25; 9:27b; 11:31 ff.), and so does *Ba* (7:25).

Let us therefore examine the relation of *Ba* to chs. 8–12 more closely. At two points in the course of Section II[3] we encountered ideas of *Ba* which presuppose the existence of the first twelve verses of ch. 8. Further, the agreements in diction between just *Ba* (not Ba) and chs. 8–12 are rightly cited by Hölscher (p. 121) as proof that *Ba* presupposes the existence of chs. 8–12 (at least substantially). In this connection Hölscher rightly[4] compares (1) *miš-takkal hwēṯ* (7:8) with *hāyīṯī mēḇīn* (8:5), (2) *qeren 'oḥrī z'ērā* (7:8) with *qeren 'aḥaṯ miṣṣ'īrā* (8:9),[5] (3) the verb *slq* in 7:8 with the verb *'ly* in 8:3, 8, (4) *mmallel raḇrḇān* (7:8, 20) with *yḏabber nip̄lā'ōṯ* (11:36; cf. *wniplā'ōṯ yašḥīṯ*,[6] 8:24), (5) *'aḏ 'iddān 'iddānīn up̄lag̅ 'iddān* (7:25) with *lmō'ēḏ mō'ḏīm wāḥeṣī* (12:7), and probably (6) *qaddīšīn* (7:21 f., by the side of *qaddīše 'elyōnīn*, which Ba employs exclusively) with *'am qḏōšīm* (8:24; cf. *'am qoḏeš*, 12:7) and (7) *wyiṯyahḇūn bīḏeh* (7:25) with *wnittan byāḏō* (11:11).

No. 5 is of special importance for determining the authorship of *Ba*, because in this case the passage compared in 8–12 is itself demonstrably secondary. The original apocalypse of 10–12, which I shall henceforth call Bc, certainly ends with 12:4. In answer to Daniel's prayers and abstinence (10:2 f., 12), and because he is 'greatly beloved' (10:19), he has been made a party to the secrets of 'that which is writ in the book of truth' (10:21) but is now cautioned to 'keep the words a secret and seal the book until the time of the last phase,'[7] so that then 'the many may seek and knowledge increase' (12:4).[8] He has fully understood the revelation. Were the latter incomprehensible, then (a) the blandishments and promises we have just cited (10:2, 12, 19, 21) would have been a mockery, and (b) there would be no point in sealing and hiding it until the final phase, since it would be at least as incomprehensible to others as to Daniel. But a new trait is added in 12:5–10, 13,[9] or *Bc*. Daniel, who has hitherto been alone with his angelus revelator (angelus interpres is hardly appropriate in Bc), beholds two kindred beings and hears them ask the former how long the final phase (*qēṣ*) is to last; to which the other replies under oath that 'after a year,[10] (two) years, and a half all these things shall end.' But Daniel is at a loss to understand the whole conversation, and his request for enlightenment is refused on the ground that 'the words are hidden and sealed until the time of the final phase.' Note how the words 'hidden and sealed,' borrowed from v. 4, where they mean just that, have acquired the figurative sense of 'obscure and mysterious.'

My impression is that this new sense is meant to be imposed upon v. 4 too; for if the entire revelation was to be kept literally hidden and sealed from the public, what harm was there in explaining any part of it privately to Daniel? In any case, the '3½ years paragraph' in ch. 12 (=*Bc*) is as surely secondary as the '3½ years strand' in ch. 7 (=*Ba*). For the '2300 mornings and evenings strand' in ch. 8 (=*Bb*), which just like *Bc* (a) introduces a time-limit for the religious persecution by means of a conversation between 'holy ones' and (b) turns an order to Daniel to keep his revelation secret from others until the advent of the distant time to which it refers into a withholding of enlightenment from Daniel himself, has for the most part already been recognized as secondary by Noth (160–1). That is because here it is for the most part ***worked into*** the texture of the original apocalypse (=Bb). Of that part of it which is merely ***appended to*** the original apocalypse Noth as a matter of fact has failed to detect the secondary character; and on the other hand he has wrongly included in the secondary expansion v. 26b, which is a perfect complement to 8:17b and a perfect parallel to 12:4. Let us therefore determine for ourselves the exact extent of *Bb.*

First of all, 8:13–14 is definitely not presupposed by 8:15–25, 26b. In v. 15, 'when I beheld the vision' refers naturally to the antics of the ram and the he-goat in vv. 2–12, and is not natural if an audition of a conversation between two invisible 'holy ones' such as we have in vv. 13–14 immediately precedes. Similarly the opening and closing formulas of the interpreting angel's exposition (vv. 17b, 26b) seem to cry warningly: 'Pay no attention to vv. 13–14. Daniel has asked for and been accorded an explanation of a spectacle, or pantomime, not of a dialog.' Moreover, in the original text (v. 24) 'holy ones' means Jews (as in ch. 7), not, as in v. 13, angels. V. 26a, on the other hand, unmistakably refers back to 'the revelation[11] about evening and morning which was *uttered*,' which is of course those very two verses 13–14. As for v. 27, 27a may be original; but 27b, with the same peculiar use of *mar'ē* as in v. 26a and with Daniel uncomprehending, in contradiction to the obvious intention of Bb that he should comprehend[12] but not broadcast,[13] is surely not Bb but *Bb.* [Have vv. 13–14 crowded out an original verse? One would have expected some feature in the vision to correspond to v. 25bβ.]

The case of v. 16 is less simple, and that of vv. 18–19 still less.

V. 16, however, is awkward in a number of ways. (1) First of all, what does *mar'ē* mean in this verse? If 'vision,' why is this concept expressed by *mar'ē* just here in contrast to *ḥāzōn* in vv. 1, 2, 15, 17, 26b? If 'revelation,' including revelation by means of words, then it clearly presupposes vv. 13–14 and belongs with these and the other verses we have already assigned to *Bb.* (2) Without this verse, we should have inferred from v. 15 that the vision came to an end with v. 12, and that the 'man' appeared to Daniel — not in a vision but in person — as he pondered his visionary trip to Susa back in his chamber in Babylon. Only v. 16 compels us to make the coming of the interpreting angel part of Daniel's experience of a visionary translocation to the Eulaeus Gate[13a] of Susa. And this is very awkward, because the angel himself refers to the vision as something outside himself (vv. 17, 26b). It is therefore my opinion that *mar'ē* in v. 16 does mean 'revelation' in general, and that v. 16 is to be added to the verses we have already assigned to *Bb*.

But without v. 16 the angel of ch. 8 is not only no part of a vision but — like the corresponding figure in Bc — anonymous. Consequently 9:21 presupposes ch. 8 with v. 16 in it. If therefore v. 16 is secondary, it must be from the same hand as wrote ch. 9 (=Bd). Of the other verses in ch. 8 which we have thus far assigned to *Bb*, this is true in any case. The novel idea introduced by them, as by the passage in ch. 12 which we assigned above to *Bc*, is the exact duration of the religious persecution. Now, a chronological scheme of the entire period of atonement thru suffering which had begun for Daniel's people and his holy city (9:24) in the days of Jeremiah is the whole content and purpose of Bd (ch. 9 minus the interpolated prayer vv. 4–20), and it culminates in just the religious persecutions of Antiochus, which it limits to half a septennium (9:27b). This round figure agrees perfectly with the 'year, (two) years, and half a year' of 7:25 and 12:7 (which is likewise a round figure) and is entirely compatible with the more exact figure of '2300 evening and morning sacrifices,' or 1150 days, of 8:14.[14]

In addition to common ideas, Bd shares with *Ba*, *Bb* and *Bc* their secondary character. Ba, Bb, and Bc have each a well marked conclusion: 7:28, 8:26b (with or without 27a), and 12:4 respectively. Only Bd has none. The common ideas and the common secondary character between them leave little room for doubt about the common authorship of Bd, *Ba*, *Bb* (at least the parts of it thus far isolated), and *Bc*. By means of 8:16 and the words 'and the man Gabriel whom I had seen in the vision the time before' in 9:21 the common author has also established continuity between ch. 8 and ch. 9. (Continuity between chs. 7 and 8 exists in virtue of 8:1bβ.)

Has he made any attempt to forge a similar link between ch. 9 and chs. 10–12? Not, to be sure, by introducing the name Gabriel. In fact he has continued to say 'the man robed in linen' even in his appendix, 12:5–10, 13 (see 12:6, 7). But if I am not mistaken he has endeavored to hint in a subtle way that this linen-clad one is identical with his Gabriel. 10:20–11:2a is a well known tangle. One solution that is to be discouraged from the start is the elimination of so original a datum as 11:1a without being able to account for its presence. My suggestion is that of these verses only 10:20–21 are original, and that 21b originally preceded 21a. The order of these clauses was then reversed for the purpose of adding to 21b the continuation (11:1, slightly emended): 'and I since the first year (rd. משנת) of Darius the Mede have been standing (rd. עֹמֵד; the present reading is due to contamination by the preceding word) by him as a helper and strengthener.' In other words, to the explanation which we have in 10:12–14 of the *three weeks'* delay (10:3) in the response to Daniel's appeal for enlightenment, there is added here an explanation of the *three or more years'* interval that has elapsed since the visit of Gabriel (9:1, 21),[15] with whom the speaker is thus made to identify himself — one can guess by whom.[15a] And since 10:21a has now been separated from 11:2b ff., which it introduces, by a verse and a half, it is repeated in the form of the variant 11:2a.

Let us leave for a while Bd and his interpolations in Ba, Bb, and Bc and consider these three basic apocalypses and their relations to one another. Ba, we have seen, was written between 175 and 167, Bb and Bc in 166 or 165. There are no very substantial discrepancies either between Ba and Bb[16] or between Ba and Bc; but there are between Bb and Bc, notably in their different applications of one prophetic text: Hab 2:2–3. The proper sense of this passage may be paraphrased thus: 'You are about to receive an oracle (*ḥāzōn*). Commit it to writing, and write it plainly so that anyone may read it at a glance. For this oracle (the omission of the article is poetic) is (not for the immediate future but) a witness[17] for an[18] appointed time and a testifier[19] for the end of a[18] period. But it is a true witness. Its fulfilment is set for a distant date, but it is absolutely certain. It will not remain outstanding a day after it falls due.' Now let us see to what uses this passage, especially the first six Hebrew words of v. 3, are put by Bb and Bc respectively.

Bb modifies the original sense very little. In Dan 8:17b, and 26b (on 19b see further on) the phrase of Hab 2:3a is applied even more literally than in its original context, since the *ḥāzōn* referred to is an actual vision (not a verbal oracle). It is, moreover, not a vision that is about to be vouchsafed (like the oracle in Habakkuk) but one that already has been vouchsafed. Nevertheless these passages agree with Hab 2:3a in making *ḥāzōn* the starting-point. They may be paraphrased thus: 'You have just been shown a *ḥāzōn*. Well, it relates to the time of the end (*qēṣ*).'

Bc, on the other hand, imposes a new meaning on every one of the key words of Hab 2:3a. Its starting-point is not *ḥāzōn* but *mō'ēd*. 10:14b; 11:27b, 35b may be paraphrased thus: 'You know of course that there is a *mō'ēḏ*. Well, it still holds in store quite a lot of *ḥāzōn* (without article, 10:14b) and a *qēṣ* (11:27b, 35b; cf. end of 35a).' In other words, *mō'ēḏ*, *ḥāzōn*, and *qēṣ* have here acquired the respective senses of 'term of the present dispensation,'[20] 'events scheduled to take place during the said term,' and 'final phase of the said term.' These misunderstandings[21] were favored by the poetic omission of the article before *ḥāzōn* in Hab 2:2–3 and by the masoretic reading *'ōḏ* 'yet, still,' which our borrower evidently already had before him in Hab 2:3a in place of the original *'ēḏ* 'witness.'[22]

It seems rather unlikely that an author would parody himself in this way, and the other differences between Bb and Bc are not calculated to dispel one's doubts. Here a vision and an interpretation by an angel, both brief and to the point; there a long recapitulation of the contents of 'the book of truth' (10:21a) by an angel,[23] afterwards remembered verbatim by Daniel. Here simply 'a man,'[24] there 'a man robed in linen, with a girdle of fine gold from Ophir(?) round his waist, his body gleaming like topaz, his face like lightning, his eyes like lamps of fire, his arms and legs like the color of burnished bronze, and the sound of his voice like the sound of roaring.' Here only the year of the revelation (8:1), there the month and day as well (10:4). Here a spontaneous vision, there a lecture in response to elaborate preparations (10:2–3).[25] Here a sparing use of Scriptural phrases, and in their proper meaning, there a cento of quotations, sometimes in quite novel significations. Here relative freshness, there dry erudition and a maximum of artificiality.

In short, I feel compelled to recognize as more probable the hypothesis that Bc is not from the same hand as Bb. It is to some extent modeled on it, to be sure, both in taking Hab 2:3a for its theme (tho as we have seen in a new sense) and in purporting to have been hidden until quite recently. For 8:26b and 12:4 to my mind preclude Bb and Bc having circulated from the very beginning as appendices to the book of Daniel. They purport to be by the hero of Daniel A, but they do not purport to have been published at the same time as Daniel A. They must at first have circulated independently of Daniel A, and possibly for a time independently of each other. But even if Bc was not from the beginning composed as a continuation of Bb, it must have been appended to it pretty early. For it seems to me that two verses in ch. 8 were interpolated by the author of Bc. The passage 8:18–19 is suspicious on more than one count. In v. 17 Daniel has already fallen upon his face and the visitor has already spoken an introductory sentence. But in v. 18 Daniel lies face downwards again and is raised up — without having been raised up before he lies down again — and in v. 19 the visitor speaks another introductory sentence, almost identical with the first. Moreover, the verb for 'to lie down' in v. 18—in contrast to the one in v. 17—is nowhere else used in this sense except in 10:9.[25a] Also, it is just in ch. 10 that Daniel (as in 8:18) drops upon his face upon hearing the messenger's voice (not, as in 8:17 at the sight of him). And in 8:19, we have (a) again an identification of Antiochus with the Assyrian rod of the Lord's anger of Isa 10,[26] and (b) Hab 2:3a alluded to in a manner suspiciously reminiscent of Bc. What with the complete superfluity of vv. 18–19, these puzzling features lead me to conclude that they are from the hand of Bc, and that 19b is to be read *kī lammō'ēḏ qēṣ*[27] and rendered 'for there is a final phase to the period' (of the divine displeasure, cf. v. a); exactly like 11:27bβ and 11:35, except that *'ōḏ* 'yet' is not expressed.

Within *Bb*, therefore, I distinguish *Bb^c*, comprising vv. 18–19 and *Bb^d*, comprising vv. 13–14, 16, 26a, 27b.

Ba's identity with Bb is not precluded, but neither is it probable.[27a] Bd, finally, can't be identical with the author of any of the three texts he supplements.

Whereas Bb and Bc are, as observed above, shown by their concluding formulas to have been intended originally to be published separately from Daniel A, the conclusion of Ba does not preclude, and its content—ch. 2 brought up to date—rather favors, its having been produced originally as an appendix to Daniel A. It is probable, however, that it was *also* circulated apart from Daniel A and was combined with Bb and Bc, perhaps from the moments of their respective appearances. At any rate, the fact that Bd's work of supplementation extends to every part of Daniel B but is also confined to Daniel B can be explained most satisfactorily on the assumption that Daniel B was once a book by itself.[27b]

After Bd had inserted his independent apocalypse (ch. 9) and his interpolations in the other three, first 12:11 and then 12:12 were added—it is hard to say whether by Bd or by one or two other writers; it is also difficult to say whether the prayer 9:4–20 was interpolated earlier or later than 12:11–12 or between the addition of 12:11 and that of 12:12.

C. Combination and Partial Translation

Within a generation after the Maccabean revolt, Daniel B was joined to Daniel A; and around the year 140, when the purport of the former was still understood by many, the whole was accorded recognition as part of the national heritage. It was probably with a view to gaining this recognition that 1:1–2:4a and chs. 8–12 were translated into Hebrew. (For proof of the Aramaic original of these portions see Section V.)

That Daniel B was originally composed in Aramaic thruout is probably due to the accident that the man Daniel was only known from the Aramaic story-book Daniel A. For this reason Ba, which was written as an appendix to Daniel A (tho it was *also* circulated separately), was likewise composed in Aramaic, and Bb, Bc, and Bd followed suit. Were it not for these special circumstances, it would have been more natural for what purported to be ancient prophecy to be composed in Hebrew (and by the way, I do not doubt but Hebrew was still spoken locally in the second century B.C.E.). As it was, what with the revival of nationalism in the Maccabean age, the apocalypses, after having been composed in Aramaic, were, with the exception of ch. 7, translated into Hebrew for the purpose of making the book acceptable as Holy Writ. It was not necessary to translate 2:4b–6:29, because this section could purport to report the conversations of which it consists in the language in which they were held. (Compare the adverb *'rāmīṯ* 'in Aramaic' by which the section is introduced.) It is more difficult to account for the retention of the Aramaic in ch. 7. Dalman,[28] who believed (mirabile dictu) that the Aramaic of ch. 7 was a translation from Hebrew, and (mirabilius dictu) that the Hebrew of chs. 8–12 was original, thought that in order to silence attacks upon the authenticity of Daniel B at a time when it was still a comparative newcomer, the language of B had been extended to the beginning of A and that of A to the beginning of B (=ch. 7). In this Dalman was followed by Torrey 1909 and Montgomery. Since there is not a trace of a Hebrew substratum in ch. 7 and an unmistakable Aramaic substratum in chs. 8–12 as well as 1:1–2:4a (see Section V), the hypothesis is untenable in that form. But may not ch. 7 *have been left untranslated from the Aramaic* so that A might be linked to B by a linguistic bond? It is at least conceivable. But it does not preclude another factor: namely, that ch. 7, because it was appended to Daniel A from the beginning (in addition to being published apart from it — for it was while circulating with the other apocalypses that it received the *Ba* verses, as explained above) was read in times of relative calm as as well as of persecution, and was therefore too well known in Aramaic for translation to be advisable.

And now let us try to appreciate the difficulties with which the translator had to contend. They were very minor in 1:1–2:4a, which is simple narrative. Consequently what he has produced there, tho not a model of Hebrew style — one does not consistently say 'years three' and 'years ten' or 'these children, the four of them' (1:17; cf. 3:23 and Ahikar papyri l. 67), or *miqṣāṯ* (1:15, 18; cf. Aram. *liqṣāṯ*, 4:26) for *miqqeṣ*, and so on, all in the space of one short chapter — does not convey wrong meanings or no meaning except in the doubtful *nihyṯā*; on which see Section V C 6.

But the case is very different in chs. 8–12 because the problem was so different. Suppose that in the hour of France's distress in the spring of 1918, when the military picture was very bleak, there came to light an apocalypse, purporting to have been written by Napoleon in Saint Helena, which, in allusive language, gave in the form of a prediction a brief sketch of European history from 1820 thru 1917 (the period of 1914–1917 being covered in some detail), followed by a genuine prediction of an Allied march on Berlin and occupation of Germany for twenty years and a permanent annexation by France of Germany west of the Rhine. Suppose also that the reading of this apocalypse was rendered harder by its being available only in manuscript. And suppose, finally, that in 1947 such a manuscript was translated into English by an American university man of the class of 1947 who knew French fairly well but little modern history and had only average skill as a translator. In the resulting English version we might expect to find passages like this: 'In the largest of the barbarian states there shall arise a figure from the nether regions (instead of "of iron," *de fer* mistaken for *d'enfer*). He shall gain the favor of his prince; and they shall rob the land of civilization of two provinces, and shall unite all the barbarians in one nation. But the prince's successor shall be a blemished person who esteems himself as a soldier and a statesman, and he shall chase his minister with iron (*il chassera son ministre de fer*), etc.' Strange to say, the closer he came to his own age, the more our translator would be likely to err, because the text would be full of allusions which could only be understood by persons who were either old enough to have followed the events of 1914–18 (when our student was still unborn) fairly intelligently or had made a special study of the period. Otherwise what would they do, for example, with the diving chariot (U-boat) that shall sink a floating palace (the Lusitania) and incense a professor (Wilson)?

That the Hebrew of Daniel is analogous,[29] and often incomprehensible until one gets behind it to the underlying Aramaic text, will be shown in the next Section.

V

THE HEBREW OF DANIEL AS A TRANSLATION

That the Hebrew portions of Daniel (i. e. chs. 1–2:4a; 8–12) are, with the exception of the obvious interpolation 9:4–20,[1] translated from Aramaic originals is a hypothesis of long standing, but was only demonstrated by Zimmermann 1938 and 1939.[2] As Baumgartner observes,[3] not all of Zimmermann's arguments are cogent, and I shall have occasion to criticize some of them in the course of this Section, but some are so telling that they suffice to establish his thesis. Such, for example, are his observations that in 10:8 the phrase *whōḏī nehpaḵ ʿālai* 'my splendor changed' is not merely a translation but a mistranslation of *wzīwai yištannōn ʿlai*, 7:28 (cf. also 5:9), since it wrongly takes the Aramaic *zīw* in the first instead of the second of its two senses of 'splendor' and 'appearance,'[4] and that in 11:33, 35 the Hebrew root *kšl* again represents the first instead of the second of the two meanings of the Aramaic *tql*: 'to stumble' and 'to weigh, test'[5] (cf. 5:27, and see above Section III end). The first of these mistakes, to be sure, might be committed by a person who thought in Aramaic even if he were not translating from a written Aramaic original; but the second can not very well have been committed by an author — who would have known that it was *tql* in the sense of 'to weigh' that he had in mind and would surely have realized that the Hebrew for that is not *kšl* but *šql*—but only by a translator, who mistook the author's intention. Convincing are also his remarks that only a translator, or at least a barbarian, would have said *bimʿaṭ gōy* (11:23) 'with not much nation,' whether he meant *bimʿaṭ ʿam* 'with few troops' or anything else;[6] and that not even a barbarian but only a translator could have said *wniṣdaq qoḏeš* (8:14). As Zimmermann points out,[7] not only does this phrase represent a poor attempt to render an Aramaic *wyizkē quḏšā* 'the sanctuary shall triumph' but the latter in turn probably represents a confusion[8] — visual or at least mental — of *wyiḏkē* (or *wyiddakī*)[9] *quḏšā* 'the sanctuary will become clean (*or* be cleansed).' Still less is it possible to explain otherwise than by the thoughtlessness of a translator, who is not identical with the author, the phrase *ma'ḇīr nōḡēś heḏer malḵūṯ* (11:20); which is practically meaningless except as a clue to [10]מהעדי[11] שלטן יקר[12] ומלכו 'one deprived of dominion, glory, and sovereignty.'[13] To cite one more example, it is obviously a correct observation[14] that in *whannišbereṯ* (8:22) the article represents an Aramaic *dī* taken as a relative particle (which in Hebrew is rendered by the article before participles) instead of as the conjunction 'that' (as in *wḏī ḥzaiṯā*, 2:41, 43). The verb in the original was probably the peil *tḇīraṯ* which because of its resemblance to the passive participle of the peal, *tḇīrā*, was rendered by the participle of the niphal in Hebrew.

Overwhelming additional proof will be found in the following pages.

A. Antiochus Epiphanes' Measures Against the Jewish Religion in Chs. 11 and 8

1. *In chapter 11.*

The portion of ch. 11 that deals with Epiphanes' sacrilege and religious persecution is vv. 29–39. Within it there occurs three times the word *mā'ōz* 'fortress, stronghold,' once (v. 31) in the singular and twice (38, 39) in the plural. But all one has to do to convince oneself that all such meanings are out of the question in this pericope is to contrast their appropriateness in vv. 1, 7, 10, 19. What the author wanted to say where we read *mā'ōz* or *mā'uzzīm* in the sacrilege pericope can only be discovered by (i) asking oneself what general sense might be suitable in all three cases,

(ii) comparing all pertinent data from within and without the book of Daniel, and (iii) discovering a suitable Aramaic word which a translator could have taken to be equivalent to Hebrew *mā'ōz* or *mā'uzzīm*.

(i) The underlying word must be some expression meaning *the Jewish people*. Because —

(a) In v. 39 *mā'uzzīm* is clearly the opposite of *'am* (so vocalize with others) *'lōh nēḵār* 'people of a strange god.' As is well known, the reference is to Epiphanes' colonizing Judean cities, especially the Akra (=citadel) of Jerusalem, with pagans (1 Macc. 1:33; 3:36, 45). 'Walled cities of fortresses' would be an inane tautology and would leave unsaid the most important thing of all, namely that the walled cities in question are not in Commagene or Media, and inhabited by idolators anyway, but Jewish towns in Judea.

(b) Since (1) even those who don't realize that *mā'uzzīm* in v. 39 is a designation of the Jews recognize that 'the walled cities of *mā'uzzīm*' are in fact Jewish cities, the 'God of *mā'uzzīm*' in the preceding verse would be unlikely to be a pagan god for that reason alone. There are plenty of others. (2) *'Al kannō* can not mean 'instead of him' because if one were saying 'instead' at all one would have to say 'instead of *them*,' since v. 37 names many gods. It is no rebuttal to say that 'instead of him' means 'instead of the god of his fathers'; because the expression *'lōhē 'ḇōṯāw* in v. 37 (α) is too far removed and (β) means 'the *gods* of his fathers.' (Contrast 2:23!) For a *single* god only the *singular* of Aram. *'lāh*, Heb. *'lōh*, is employed in Daniel (vv. 37b, 38a, 38b, 39). (3) Possibly some freak in the Greekling camp, more Hellenic than the Hellenes, would have been exercised over the king's favoring Roman *'līlīm* 'nothings' over Greek, or new ones over old. But our author and his readers would not even have known enough about Jupiter Capitolinus, or the goddess Roma, or what not, and about Antiochus's relation to them, to recognize such an allusion; and if they had, they wouldn't have cared a button. Only that Antiochus (by calling himself a god) was disrespectful to all gods did interest them, because it explained his lack of reverence for the God of Zion.[14a] (4) But though arrogant towards his ancestral gods, Antiochus as a matter of fact never exchanged them for others. By preferring, in the latter part of his reign, the figure of Zeus Olympius to that of Apollo seated upon the omphalos for his coins, he did not repudiate the worship of Apollo any more than his four immediate predecessors had repudiated him by not representing him on their coins at all; and neither did he repudiate the worship of Zeus Olympius — with whom he in fact identified himself — by building a temple to Jupiter Capitolinus. Some day people will marvel that this refutation should have been necessary. (5) In the parallel text 8:10–12 we are told first how Epiphanes magnifies himself over 'the host of heaven . . . and the stars,' meaning 'the heavenly bodies, especially as the objects of heathen worship, and as the celestial rulers of the world,'[15] and then — climactically — how he flouts 'the Prince of the host,' and substitutes an alien cult for his *upon his stand*.[15a] It is the same in 11:36–38, where vv. 37 and 38 do but explicate v. 36.

Consequently, if one leaves the text of v. 38 unchanged one must take the first *yḵabbeḏ* as a euphemism: 'He will defy, or insult, the God of *mā'uzzīm upon his station*.' However, I frankly don't believe *yḵabbeḏ* can have been used first in this sense in 38a and then in its ordinary and natural one in 38b. I believe *'al kannō yḵabbeḏ* in 38a is a — superior — variant of *yḵabbeḏ* in 38b, and that it has ousted the word — perhaps ינאץ or יבזה — (or the words) that originally followed *mā'uzzīm*. And in that case the sense of the verse is: 'And the God of *mā'uzzīm* will he despise, and *upon His stand* he will honor a god that his fathers knew not etc.'[15b] But either way, it is not at Antiochus's honoring a god that his fathers knew not that the writer is aghast, but at his doing so *upon the stand* — the altar — *of the God of the Jews*. Not that he would have been a whit less horrified had the impious prince honored his national gods there, but it just happens that every bit of information we have about the pagan cult practiced in the sanctuary of Zion during the persecution goes to show that it was not Greek but Semitic, and that its chief divinity was but a paganized version of the Jewish 'God of Heaven' (Neh 2:4, etc.); whose name was interpreted as *Zeus Olumpios* to the Greeks, but who no more assumed Olympian traits than did other Oriental deities which were nominally identified with Greek deities in the Hellenistic age.[16] The Jews could not accept the paganized 'god of heaven' or 'lord of heaven' [it has been suggested that *šiqqūṣ šōmēm* — 9:27; 11:31; 12:11 — is a cacophony of Heb. *'lōh* (*ba'al*) *šāmaim* or Aram. *'lāh* (*b'el*) *šmain*], but they knew that he was not a Greek god either.

(c) As for v. 31, it will be admitted that something meaning the Jewish people would be not inappropriate in the position occupied by *mā'ōz*. But here it is the method of consulting external evidence that will pay the biggest dividends.

(ii) Dan 11:31b reads as follows:

and they shall profane the temple . . . , and remove the daily sacrifice, and set up an[17] appalling abomination.

And in 1 Macc 1 we read:

(44) And the king sent letters by messengers unto Jerusalem and the cities of Judah commanding them to follow the laws of the strangers of the land: (45) to withhold burnt offerings, and sacrifice, and drink offering from the sanctuary, and *profane* (bebēlosai<Heb. ulḥallēl) sabbaths and festivals, (46) and to *pollute sanctuary and saints* (mianai hagiasma kai hagious); (47) to set up altars, and groves, and idols, and sacrifice swine's flesh and unclean beasts, (48) and leave their sons uncircumcised, *and render themselves abominable with all manner of uncleanness and profanation* (bdeluxai tas psukhas autōn en panti akathartōi kai bebēlōsei<Heb. [approximately] ulšaqqeṣ 'et napšōtēhem bkol ṭāmē [*or* ṭum'ā] upiggūl [*or* wḥillūl, *or* wāḥōl?]);[18] (49) to the end that they might forget the

> Law and change all statutes . . . (54) And on the fifteenth day of Kislev, in the hundred and forty-fifth year,[19] *they set up an appalling abomination upon the altar* (ōikodomēsan bdelugma erēmōseōs epi to thusiastērion <Heb. nāṯnū šiqqūṣ šomēm 'al hammizbēḥ) and in the cities of Judah round about they constructed pagan altars (bomous).

When, therefore, it is further recalled that in Dan 7 the Jews are called 'saints (of the Most High)' and in 8:24 'people of saints' (cf. further 12:7 'holy people'), we ought to have no hesitation in asserting that *mā'ōz* in 11:31 (cf. 1 Macc 1:46) and *mā'uzzīm* in 11:38, 39 must be erroneous renderings of an Aramaic word meaning 'saints,' provided an Aramaic word can be found which has this meaning but — unlike the *qaddīšīn* of ch. 7 — could be mistaken for another Aramaic word meaning 'fortress' or 'fortresses.'

(iii) Such a word is חֲסַיִן (plural of חֲסֵא). As is well known, this word is common in Syriac (sing. *ḥsē/ḥasyā*, pl. *ḥsēn/ḥsayyā*) and is possibly represented in the text of the Carpentras stela (but see *NSI*, 206). In Jewish usage, however, it has hitherto been known only as the name of the sect of the 'Εσσαῖοι or 'Εσσηνοί.[19a] חֲסַיִן could easily be confused with both חֲסֵן 'stronghold' and חִסְנִין 'strongholds' (cf. Syr *ḥesnā* 'stronghold'; *ḥusnā*, the same, in Targum to Ps 31:3; also *ḥisnā* 'the strength' in Dan 2:37), especially by a translator who had encountered the latter and cognate words repeatedly in the same chapter.

For —

(a) In 11:1[20] ואני ˹משנת˺ אחת לדריוש המדי ˹עמד˺ למחזיק ולמעוז לו goes back to something like this: ואנה מן שנת חדה לדריוש [21]מדיא קאם לְמְגַבַּר וְלִמְחַסֵּן לה 'and I since the first year of Darius the Mede have been standing as a strengthener and fortifier for him.'

Note. למגבר, if correctly reconstructed, is a play on the supposed speaker's name גבריאל.[22] The Hebrew root *ḥzq* occurs repeatedly between 10:18 and 11:7, and does not necessarily represent the same Aramaic root every time, but that it renders an Aramaic *gbr* at least in some cases is not improbable in itself and is likely for special reasons not only in this verse but also in 11:6. For although the last two clauses in this verse are a well known crux, it is certain that they refer to the violent deaths of Berenice and Antiochus II and their infant child at the hands of Laodice and Seleucus II (whom Laodice had borne to Antiochus II). Now, the vague expression 'those that brought her' (if correct) may mean the suite that accompanied Berenice from Egypt or somebody else, but והילדה ומחזיקה would seem to mean 'and her child and her husband.' והילדה is either to be emended to וְיַלְדָּהּ, or to be read וְהַ־יַּלְדָּה[23] or perhaps וְהַיָּלְדָה 'and he whom she hath borne' (<ודי ילדת — better>ואשר ילדה); while *umaḥzīqāh* seems to be a mistranslation of *wḡaḇrāh* 'and her husband' — another example of *ḥzq*<*gbr*.

(b) In 11:7 ויבא אל החיל ויבא במעוז מלך הצפון ועשה בהם והחזיק goes back to something like this: וידבר[a] לחילֵהּ[b] וְיֵעֹל בחסני[c] מלכא די צפונא ויעבד[d] בהון ויגבר 'and he shall lead his army and enter the strongholds of the king of the north and shall do his pleasure[d] in them and prevail.'

Notes. [a]The corresponding Hebrew word is therefore to be vocalized *wyāḇē* (not *wyāḇī*, since the translator regularly substitutes the jussive for the indicative). — [b]The translator took the ל as the preposition 'to' instead of as the exponent of the determinate direct object, and the final ה as the sign of the emphatic state instead of as the pronominal suffix. — [c]Emend also the Hebrew to *bmā'uzzē*; note the following *ba*hem ... *'lōhē*hem ... *nsīḵē*hem ... *ḥemdāṯa*m. — [d]But see below para. (h).

(c) In 11:10b וישב ויתגרו[a] עד מעזה[a] probably goes back to ויתוב[b] ויתגרי עד חסנה 'and he (Seleucus II's son Antiochus III)[c] shall fight back to his (the king of the south's, now Ptolemy IV) stronghold.'[d]

Notes. [a–a]Read ויתגרה עד מעזה with qre, or else ויתגָרֵי עד מעֻזֹּה — cf. the restored Aramaic original. — [b]Of course ויהפך, or ויהדר, or ויחזר, is also possible. The same is true mutatis mutandis in almost every case where the Hebrew has the root שוב. — [c]In v. 10a read with Baumgartner *BHK*[3] ובנו יתגרה ואסף; cf. the following verbs. — [d]To make the context clearer note that in v. 8b והוא is almost certainly a mistranslation of והא 'and lo' and שנים and ממלך either false readings or false renderings for שֵׁנִית and מלך respectively. Vv. 8b–9 ought therefore to have been rendered: 'and behold the king of the north (Seleucus II) shall rise a second time, (9) and he shall penetrate the kingdom of the king of the south (Ptolemy III) and return to his own land.' The Aramaic original of v. 8b was something like והא תנינות יקום מלכא די צפונא. The interjection הא seems to have been misunderstood again in 10:20, being there mistaken for the interrogative ה. Correct the first word to הֵן ידעת<הא ידעת.

(d) In 11:12 והפיל רבבות ולא יעוז probably goes back to [a]ורבון יהנפל ולא יַחְסֵן 'and he (Ptolemy IV) shall cause myriads to fall (at the battle of Raphia, 217) but shall not take possession.'

Note. [a]*Ribbwān*, pl. of *ribbō*. In 7:10 the qre substitutes **ribbān* as if from **ribbā* (Heb. *rbābā*).

(e) In 11:19 וישב פניו למעוזי ארצו goes back to ויהדר אנפוהי לחסני ארעה.

But —

(f) 11:31, וזרעים ממנו יעמדו וחללו המקדש המעוז והסירו התמיד ונתנו השקוץ משומם goes back to something like [a]ו(א)דרעין מנה [b]יקומון [c]וי(ה)פסון מקדש [d]וחסין וי(ה)עדון [e]תמידא ויתנון [f]שקוץ שמם[f]. 'And forces shall arise from him and shall profane sanctuary and saints[g] and abolish the daily sacrifice and set up an appalling abomination.'

Notes. [a]For the form with prothetic aleph see Ezra 4:23, where the word means '(physical) force, coercion.' In Dan 11:15, 22, and 31 it means 'forces' in the sense of 'armies'; in v. 6 perhaps 'strength.' Note in our verse the plural *-īm* in imitation of the Aramaic *-īn*.[24] — [b]This form points to the probable explanation of the Hebrew *ya'modū* instead of *ta'modnā* or *ya'modnā* (see 8:22 and sub-Section C para. 1 thereon, and the analagous phenomena in 11:15, 22). It is because the Aramaic *drā'* is masculine. For a Jewish text cf. Targum Onqelos (ed. Berliner) to Deut. 26:8 ביד תקיפא ובדרע מרמם, for Syriac cf. the Peshitta to the same passage (where all four words are in the emphatic state, which is normal for Syriac). — [c]The Palestinian Aramaic word for 'to profane' is the (h)aphel of *pss*, not of *ḥll*. I should nevertheless have considered both verbs equally plausible, were there not verses of which the Hebrew can only have arisen from Aramaic originals containing the former. See below, Section V A 2. — [d]The Hebrew has the article with both substantives, but I've already pointed out that the translator was not clear about the relation between the Hebrew article and the Aramaic emphatic state.[25] The conjunction before the second substantive has dropped out from the Hebrew; but cf. below, Section V A 2 on the parallel in ch. 8, and cf. *hagiasma kai hagious*, 1 Macc 1:46 (quoted above). — [e]The Hebrew word was probably employed as a technical term in the Aramaic; if a native word was used it may have been תדירא (cf. 6:17, 21). — [f–f]The Hebrew probably read השקוץ השומם, which is at least consistent, but in the original the expression was probably indeterminate; cf. 12:11 and *bdelugma erēmōseōs*, 1 Macc 1:54 (quoted above). — [g]They profaned the saints by causing them to behave in a profane manner, as is clear from the context of the identical expression in 1 Macc 1:46 (quoted above). Similarly the episode of Israel's going astray after the heathen god Baal-peor (Num 25) is introduced in Pseudo-Jonathan as follows: And Israel dwelt in a place called Shittim for the folly (*šṭūṯā*) and corruption they were guilty of there. The people began *to profane their sanctity* etc. The Aramaic expression — which is of course a midrashic epexegesis of the Hebrew ויחל (as if = וַיֵּחֶל) is לאופסא קדושתהון; read לאפסא ק׳, the abnormal spelling being due to contamination with טופסא 'image,' which occurs a little further on.

(g) 11:38, as I have already explained, should read something like ולאלה מעזים ינאץ(?) ולאלוה אשר לא ידעהו אבותיו על כנו יכבד וגו׳, the Aramaic original of which will have looked something like this: ולאלההון די חסין [a]יהקל ולאלה די לא ידעוה אבהתה על [b]מתקנה יהוקר וגו׳.

Notes. [a]Haphel of *qll*, the literal antithesis of יהוקר; cf. 1 Sam 2:30bβ. Since even the Hebrew rendering of this verb has been lost, as explained on p. 44, the precise Aramaic word is doubly difficult to determine. — [b]*Matqnā* is the regular Syriac rendering of *kan* and *mākōn*.

(h) In 11:39, finally, the Aramaic original of ועשה למבצרי מעזים [26]עַם אלוה נכר may have been, to the very letter, as follows: ויעבר לכרכי חסין עַם אלה נָכְרָי.[a]

Notes. [a]Syr has ויעבר. Syr's original rendering of the Hebrew ועשה must have been ויעבר, but whoever is responsible for the corruption sensed what the context requires. The Heb. ויעשה is certainly the result of a misreading of וַיַּעֲבֵר as וַיַּעֲבֵד. In the same way ועשה in vv. 28 and 30 certainly goes back to וַיַּעבר; cf. v. 10, where יעבר is certainly correct because ושטף ועבר (cf. v. 40) is a quotation from Isa 8:8. (Possibly the root עשי further (mis)represents the Aramaic עבר in Dan 8:12 and 11:7.) —

2. *In chapter 8.*

In 8:11–12 we must first of all, as is well known, advance the border of v. 11 just beyond *wṣāḇā*, so that this word will be joined with *miqdāšō* even as *wṣāḇā* in v. 13 is joined with *qodeš*; and we must also delete the suffix of *miqdāšō* as a dittography of the *w* of *wṣāḇā*, cf. again the corresponding phrase in v. 13. Further we must, with Theodotion, read *pāša'* for *bpāša'* in v. 12.

Next, the verbs in v. 11 are notoriously not in order. To begin with they are masculine whereas their subject is the feminine substantive *qeren* 'horn' (v. 9), and to be satisfied with the explanation that by the time the author reached v. 11 he forgot this and went over to the masculine because he was thinking of Antiochus[27] — whom, to be sure, the horn represents — is to shut one's eyes to the fact that the verbs in the following verse (v. 12) still agree with *qeren*. This, by the way, also applies to the first verb in v. 12, which, without any consonantal emendation, is to be vocalized *tinten*, an Aramaism for *titten* (cf. the masculine *yintin* in 2:16) of a sort unlikely to occur in original Hebrew composition. Preferably a *w* should be restored at the beginning of this word; so read *wṯinten*.

As a matter of fact, even those who recognize the necessity for emendation in v. 11 have not paid sufficient attention to v. 12. The gender of the verbs here is feminine as in vv. 9–10, but the tenses are no longer perfect and imperfect consecutive but imperfect and perfect consecutive. I have no doubt whatever but the author made the switch in v. 11, so that all the graphic change that is necessary here for the restoration of grammatical concord is the very slight one of ה to ת: read *ṯāḡdīl*, *ṯārīm*, and *wṯašleḵ*. Such imperfects, having the force of historic presents, are not infrequent in the Aramaic portion of Daniel (e. g., in 4:2, 31, 33; 7:16, 28), and we shall presently offer irrefragable proof that our passage — like every other Hebrew passage in Daniel except 9:4–20 — is translated from an Aramaic original.

Unfortunately, in the case of at least one of our three verbs, changing it from the masculine perfect to the feminine imperfect by correcting its initial ה to ת is only half the battle. *Wṯašleḵ*, as we have modified the third one to read, is identical with the second verb of v. 12; but whereas 'it will cast down' in v. 12 is shown to be correct by the following 'to the ground,' 'it will cast down' in v. 11 makes no sense; and a glance at the last three words in v. 13 will show that originally the third verb in v. 11 was *wṯirmos*, which has been ousted by the intrusion of *wṯašleḵ* from v. 12.

As a matter of fact, the parallels 11:31 and 12:11 suggest that the second of our corrected verbal forms, תרים, is also all right only as to gender and tense but not as to root: it would take little more than a transposition of letters to change it to תסיר. But while I think this has much in its favor, I shall not insist upon it but shall consistently write both forms side by side as alternatives, thus: תרים/תסיר.

So far so good, but we can't stop there. In vv. 11b–12, the word מכון 'establishment, base' is shown by the parallel, v. 13 end, to be superfluous where it stands, in 11bβ, whereas it is sorely needed at two other points, namely 11bα and 12aα. For say what one will, 'from him it removed the daily sacrifice' (11bα) is harsh, and 'it set up upon the daily sacrifice an offense' (12aα) is atrocious. But מכון does not fit into the syntax of 11bα and does fit in beautifully between על and התמיד in 12aα. Hither it must therefore be transferred from 11bβ, and 12aα must then be rendered 'and it set up upon ⌜the stand of⌝ the daily sacrifice an offense'; which is the perfect visionary counterpart of the historical report 'they constructed an appalling abomination upon the altar' (1 Macc 1:54) with which we are already familiar. As for 11bα, all that is necessary there is to emend וממנו 'and from him' to וממכונו 'and from its stand.' Alternatively read וּמִכַּנּוֹ, which means the same thing.[28]

In the light of the foregoing and of a few additional remarks, which we shall supply in footnotes, a revised Hebrew and English text of all of 8:7–14 may now be presented:

(7) וראיתיו מגיע אצל האיל ויתמרמר אליו ויך את האיל וישבר
את שתי קרניו ולא היה כח באיל לעמד לפניו וישליכהו ארצה
וירמסהו ולא היה מציל לאיל מידו: (8) וצפיר העזים הגדיל
עד מאד וכעצמו נשברה הקרן הגדולה ותעלנה [29]חזות(?) ארבע
תחתיה לארבע רוחות השמים: (9) ומן האחת [30]מהם [31]יצא קרן
אחת [32]מצעירה ותגדל יתר אל הנגב ואל המזרח ואל הצבי:
(10) ותגדל עד **צבא** השמים ותפל ארצה מן **הצבא** {ומן
הכוכבים?} ותרמסם: (11) [33]ועד שר **הצבא** ⌜יתגדיל וממכונו

תרים/תסיר⌝ התמיד ⌜ותרמס⌝ מקדש (12) וצבא ⌜:⌝ ⌜ותנתן⌝ על
⌜מכון⌝ התמיד [34]⌜פשע⌝ ותשלך אמת ארצה ועשתה והצליחה:
(13) ואשמעה אחד קדוש מדבר ויאמר אחד קדוש לפלמוני
המדבר עד מתי החזון התמיד ⌜מורם/מוסר⌝ [35]והפשע [36]{שמם}
תת וקדש וצבא מרמס: (14) ויאמר [37]⌜אליו⌝ עד ערב בקר אלפים
ושלש מאות ונצדק קדש:

> (7) And I saw him reach the ram, and he was moved with choler against him, and he smote the ram and broke his two horns and the ram was powerless to resist him. And he hurled him to the ground and *TRAMPLED* him *DOWN*, and there was none that could deliver the ram out of his hand. (8) Then the he-goat magnified himself mightily. But at the height of his power his[38] big horn broke off, and in its stead four stout ones came shooting up towards the four winds of heaven. (9) From one of these issued a little horn which grew mightily towards the south, the east, and the Delight.[39] (10) It grew up to the *HOST* of heaven, and flung some of the *HOST* {and the stars?} to the ground and *TRAMPLED* them *DOWN*. (11) It even magnified itself against the Prince of the *HOST*, and removed the daily sacrifice ⌜from its stand,⌝ and ⌜*trampled down*⌝ sanctuary[40] (12) and *host*; and upon ⌜the stand of⌝ the daily sacrifice it set up ⌜an offense.⌝ It hurled truth to the ground, and prospered in what it did. (13) Then I overheard an angel speaking, and another angel said to that certain one that was speaking, For how long is this vision: the daily sacrifice removed, a[41] {revolting} offense set up, and sanctuary and *host trampled*? (14) And he said ⌜unto him,⌝ For two thousand and three hundred evenings and mornings:[42] then shall the sanctuary be cleansed.[43]

Now look back and examine the matter printed in italics. It is a strange fact that each of the expressions 'host' and 'to trample down' is employed in one sense in vv. 7, 10–11a (there printed in italicized capitals) and in another in vv. 11b–13. In the former, 'to trample' of course means just that, and the 'host,' which in its first occurrence is qualified as 'of heaven' and in its second juxtaposed with 'stars' (perhaps a — correct — gloss) means 'the heavenly bodies, especially as the objects of heathen worship, and as the celestial rulers of the world.'[44] We have seen in V A 1 that in 11:36 'every god' answers to 'the host of heaven' of 8:10, and 'the God of gods' to 'the Prince of the host' of 8:11a and to 'the Prince of princes' of 8:25; while the slighted heathen gods of 11:37 again correspond to the trampled stars of 8:10, and 11:38 again speaks of Antiochus's insolence towards the God of the Jews. In 8:11b–13, on the other hand, 'host' designates the Jews. In the light of ch. 11 (on which see A 1) it must stand for 'saints,' and the next step is to realize that 'to trample' stands for 'to profane'; the former corresponding to the *mā'ōz/mā'uzzīm*<*ḥsain* of 11:31, 38, 39 (see above, V A 1), and the latter to *wḥilllū*<*wīhappsūn* of 11:31.

How, then, did 'host' and 'to trample' come to mean such different things in 8:7, 10–11a on the one hand and in 8:11b–13 on the other? Or better, why is it that they seem to be employed as unnatural figures of speech made up ad hoc (for, 'host' is not a natural metonymy for 'saints,' and 'to trample' is not a natural euphemism for 'to profane,' least of all in the sense of 'to compel holy people to behave profanely'[45]) immediately after being employed in natural and accepted significations? The answer to this question can not be found in the Hebrew text, but only in the Aramaic original which underlies it. Here is approximately how it read:

(7) וחזיתה מטא לות דכרא ואתמרמר עלוהי ומחא [45a]לתרתיהין
קרנוהי ולא הוא חיל בדכרא למקם קדמוהי ורמהי לארעא
ורפסה ולא הוא משיזב לדכרא מן ידה: (8) וצפיר עזיא רבא
לחדה, וכדי תקף תבירת קרנה רבתא [46]וסלקי [47]חֲזָיָן ארבע
חלפיה לארבע רוחי שמיא. (9) ומן חדה מנהין [48]נפקת קרן [49]חדה
זעירה, ורבת יתיר לדרומא ולמדנחא ולתשבחתא. (10) ורבת עד
חיל שמיא, והפלת לארעא מן חילא {ומן כוכביא?} ורפסת
המון. (11) [50]ועל רב חילא תתרברב; ומן [51]מתקנה תהעדא
תמידא, [52]ות(ה)פסי מקדש (12) וחסין. ותנתן על מתקן

תמידא סרחן, ותרמא [53]יציבא לארעא, ותעבד ותהצלח.
(13) ושמעת חד קדיש ממלל, ואמר חד קדיש לפלן, [54]מן די
ממלל, עד אמתי חזוא: תמידא ומהעדיי, וסרחן {שמם?} למתן,
וקדש וחסין להפסה? (14) ואמר ילה,' עד רמש צפר [55](תרין)
אלפין ותלת מאון וְיִדְכֵּא / וְיֵדְּכֵי קדש(א).

In addition to the footnotes, the following explanations are necessary. The words in large or linear type correspond to words in these respective types in the Hebrew a few pages back and to words in italicized capitals and italicized lower case in the English translation two paragraphs back. It will be seen that Hebrew רמס in majuscules corresponds to Aramaic רפס (cf. 7:7, 19), but Hebrew רמס in minuscules to Aramaic הפס (haphel of פסס) 'to profane' *misread* (or even *corrupted* to?) רפס under the influence of the preceding רפס; and that Hebrew צבא in majuscules corresponds to Aramaic חיל(א), but Hebrew צבא in minuscules to Aramaic חסין (absolute) [or חסיא (emphatic)][56] 'saints, pious ones' *misread* for (or even *corrupted* to?) חיל(א) under the influence of the preceding חיל(א). If the latter blunder seems a little far fetched, it may be pointed out that (1) it was not so much a case of misreading as of erroneous identification: finding the expression הפס חֲסִ֫ין, about whose meaning he was not sure, immediately after the expression רפס חיל, which he understood, the translator identified the former with the latter (or perhaps thought that חַסִּין 'strong' could also mean 'host'); and (2) some word meaning 'saints' is imperative in the light of the passage from 1 Macc quoted above and of Dan 11. Verse 31 of that chapter, a perfect parallel to our 11b–12a and 13bβ, reads וחללו המקדש המעוז והסירו התמיד ונתנו השקוץ משומם. Here, obviously, וי(ה)פסון has been rendered correctly because there was no neighboring form of רפס to mislead the translator (the verb רמס doesn't occur in the Hebrew of ch. 11);[57] whereas חסין, as we saw in V A 1, has been misread (or become corrupted) here too, being mistaken this time for חסן 'stronghold, citadel' because it has been preceded by this and cognate words several times earlier in the chapter.

The correct Hebrew equivalent of *ḥsain*, by the way, is of course *ḥsīḏīm*.

B. *Mar'ē* and *'Aḥrīṯ*

In the Hebrew of Daniel neither *mar'ā* nor *mar'ē* ever means 'vision.' *Mar'ā* (10:7, 8, 16) means 'spectacle, manifestation or apparition.' It is something unusual, but it is real and produces the same image on the retina of the physical eye as in the mind;[58] which can not be said, for example, of the drama of the two ruminants in ch. 8, which outside of Daniel's psyche are two groups of — as yet unborn — dynasties. As for *mar'ē*, we saw that where it has anything to do with sight it means simply 'appearance, aspect' (e. g., 10:6), but that in a number of passages it has nothing to do with sight at all but only with hearing: 8:16, 26a, 27b; 9:23; 10:1.[58a] It is true that *ḥāzōn*, properly 'vision,' often means simply oracle; but *mar'ē* never means 'vision' in Daniel and never means 'oracle' outside Daniel. The situation here is due to the fact that the Hebrew of Daniel is translated from Aramaic. In the Aramaic portion of Daniel, at 5:12, there occurs a word *'aḥwāyā* which means (1) 'declaration, explanation, solution' and (2) 'exhibition.' Obviously this word can very well have figured in the Aramaic of all of the aforementioned passages; where its first sense is required, but its second sense has been rendered—by means of *mar'ē*.

The same Aramaic *'aḥwāyā* has been mistranslated in another way in 12:8. It is evident, as Charles (p. 335–6) points out, that the Aramaic original of the last three words in that verse was מה אחוית אלין 'what is the *explanation* of these things?' but the translator (or maybe the scribe who copied the translator's *vorlage*) has misread אחרית (this word is also used in Aramaic, 2:28) for אחוית. That 'explanation' is the sense required by the context was felt by the LXX, which accordingly renders אחרית[59] by λύσις 'solution.'[60]

C. Miscellaneous Proofs of the Translation Character of the Hebrew

1. The best single proof is the alternation of *watta'moḏnā* and *ya'moḏnā* in 8:22. The hypothesis of translation accounts for it perfectly, and no other does.[61] The former corresponds to an Aramaic *wqāmī*,[62] a form without any preformative to mislead the Hebrew translator; the latter to *yqūmān*, which an unwary translator might well render according to the proportion *yqūm(ūn)* : *ya'moḏ(ū)* :: *yqūmān* : *ya'moḏnā*. He did much better in v. 4, where he simply followed the talmudic Hebrew practice of substituting the masculine plural — *ya'mḏū* — for the feminine plural.[63]

2. Incidentally I seriously doubt whether in the same verse מגוי, or even מִגּוֹי (as Lxx, Th, and Vulg render in order to make sense but did not necessarily have in their Hebrew manuscripts), is a correct reading, and still more whether it is a correct rendering of the Aramaic original. As I have already pointed out, there is in vv. 20–21 no talk of kings or nations but only of kingdoms, thus: '(2) The ram which thou sawest that had the two horns is the kingdoms[64] of Media and Persia. (21) The he-goat is the kingdoms of Greece, and the big horn that was on its forehead is the first kingdom.' It is therefore probable that the translator's Aramaic text read מן גוה and not unlikely that he ineptly rendered this by מִגַּוּוֹ — which would mean 'from its back' (cf. 1 Ki 14:9; Prov 26:3), but which he may have intended to mean the same thing as מגויתו 'from its body' — instead of by מקרבו 'from its (i. e., the first Greek kingdom's) midst.'

3. To proceed, the very root *'md* which we discussed in para. 1, apart from the preformatives it assumes in 8:22, is instructive. In the Hebrew of Daniel the verb *qwm* occurs only in 8:27. Otherwise *'md* is used indifferently for 'to stand' and 'to stand up,' exactly as *qwm* is in Aramaic. That in itself, however, is a feature not of translation Hebrew but of late (talmudic) Hebrew, just like

the hapax eirēmenon *ḥtk* (9:24). Where the choice of *'md* instead of *qwm* betrays the translator is where it corresponds to a Hebrew *qwm* in a quotation from Scripture. This is the case with 11:17bβ. Probably the last *lō* is to be omitted there with Lxx, in which case it is a quotation from Isa 7:7 'It shall not succeed and it shall not be'; if not, it is at any rate a parody on Isa 7:7. But the latter has *lo ṯāqūm*, while our verse has *lō ṯa'mōḏ*. That is not the kind of mistake that would be likely to be made by the person who applied the quotation, even if he were quoting from memory. But a Maccabean translator who saw before him in Aramaic לא תקום ולא (לה) תהוה would not necessarily know Isa 7:7 by heart, in which case he would turn it mechanically into לא תעמד ולא (לו) תהיה.

4. The word which is spelled אבל in 8:3, 6, and אובל (upon which the masoretic vocalization is based) only (at least in most codices) in 8:2 — obviously thru contamination with the following word אולי — can be nothing but the Aramaic *'aḇol/'aḇulla* (<Accad. *abullu*) 'city gate'; as was realized by Lxx and Syr. The rendering 'stream' rests upon the resemblance — not identity! — of the form in v. 2 to the rare Hebrew word *yūḇal* 'stream' and upon the existence of a river, or rather canal, Ulai-Eulaeus in the vicinity of Susa. But we have just seen how the form in v. 2 originated, and the existence of a canal Ulai does not alter the fact that א(ו)בל can only mean 'gate.' The homonymy may have arisen either, as elsewhere, thru the naming of the gate for the locality it led out to, or otherwise. However, in Palestinian Aramaic, *'aḇol* is less frequent than *tra'* (in amoraic times also *pīlē* <πύλη), and not improbably our translator failed to recognize it and therefore merely copied it; just as Theodotion, in turn, was at a loss to interpret, and therefore merely transcribed, our corrupt אובל.[64a]

5. The difficulty in the negative clauses in 8:5 and 8:27 is well known. ואין נוגע בארץ (v. 5) means 'with no one touching the ground'; whereas the sense required is 'without (his) touching the

ground,' *Hebraice* אינני נוגע בארץ . Of course it would be easy to emend the text accordingly and posit a haplography, but Baumgartner *BHK*3 ad loc. rightly calls attention to ואין מבין (v. 27). This phrase means 'with no one explaining' or 'with no one understanding'; but since Daniel has been expressly forbidden to divulge his information to anybody (v. 26b), the sense required is again 'without (my) understanding,' *Hebraice* ואינני מבין. The explanation is as follows. In Aramaic, participles are regularly negated by *lā* (see 2:43; 3:12, 16; 4:4, 6; 5:8, 23); but in Hebrew *lō* negates participles only in certain cases (e. g. neither . . . nor . . . , not . . . but . . .), otherwise the subject of the participle is negated instead, and that by means of *'ēn*. The translator, who found in his Aramaic text of v. 5 something like ולא נָגֵע בארעא, remembered to use the right Hebrew negative particle, but he did not realize that it can only negate the subject, which must consequently be expressed in Hebrew (by means of a pronominal suffix). The case of v. 27 may be slightly different. It depends on whether the original of *wā'eštōmem* was some participial expression (like *wa'nā* [*hwēṯ*] *mištōmam*) or *w'eštōmmet*. In the former case (which is perhaps the less probable), the end of the sentence was simply *wlā miśtakkāl*, and the translator committed exactly the same error as in v. 5. In the latter, the Aramaic too could not very well, at least in the first and second persons, pass over from the perfect to the participle (which does not indicate the person by its form) without expressing the subject. I therefore surmise that v. 27b in Aramaic read as follows: *w'eštōmmeṯ 'al 'aḥwāyṯa wlā 'īṯai miśtakkāl* (cf. 3:14). But it so happens that *la 'īṯai*, in the Aramaic of this period, corresponds to both *'ēn* (see 2:10) and *'ēnennī* in Hebrew (in later times Syriac, for example, has *lait* for the former and *laitai* for the latter), and the translator made the wrong choice. [And in truly idiomatic Hebrew he would not have used the participle at all but, as in 12:8, the imperfect: ולא אבין.]

6. In the same verse (8:27), the word נהייתי is meaningless. The

meaningful Aramaic word it represents is probably אֶתַּוְּהֵת (the ethpaal of תוהּ [3:24], which occurs in Syriac) 'I was dazed'; cf. 7:28b. The translator, however, did not know, or because of the imperfections of the vowelless script failed to recognize, this word and instead took it as אתהו<י>ת (one or other of the three Aramaic reflexive conjugations of הוא), which might mean 'I became' if it occurred; and knowing that the Hebrew for הוא is היהּ and that the Aramaic ethpeel (and to some extent the ethpaal and the ettaphal) is the functional equivalent of the Hebrew niphal, and perhaps remembering that a niphal of היהּ does occur (Jud 19:30; Dan 12:1), he rendered the supposed אתהו<י>ת by נהייתי.

The equally enigmatic נהיתהּ of 2:1 may similarly represent אֶתַּוְּהַת misunderstood as אתהוַית, if the former could mean 'was troubled' (of sleep).

7. Of the many esthetic jolts that punctuate a ride thru Dan 8–12 there are two of which one is like a repetition of the other. It is a bad sign for a Hebraist if the expression *nirdamtī ʿal pānai 'arṣā* does not jar him. *Nirdam* never means anything but 'to fall asleep,' yet the angel does not wake Daniel but only raises him (8:18; 10:9); and *'arṣā* expresses 'motion towards.' The sentence is therefore just as unnatural as 'I fell asleep down to the ground on my face,' followed by an indication that the speaker remained awake, would be in English. The explanation lies in the Aramaic verb *dmeḵ* or *dmuḵ*, which means 'to lie' (notably in Syriac) as well as 'to sleep.' What the author said was 'I lay down upon my face on the ground.' In Hebrew the proper word for this is *npl*, literally 'to fall' and this was evidently also the one used in Aramaic by Bb in 8:17 (cf. 2:40, 3:5, etc.). Bc, on the other hand who, we saw on pp. 36–37, is the author of 8:18–19 as well as the bulk of 10–12, evidently said *dmk* (which in the sense of 'to lie' ought properly to be rendered by *škb* in Hebrew, but here it would be best to imitate Gen 19:1bγ).

8. Montgomery rightly equates the Heb. *hmlk* of 9:1 with the

Syriac *'amleḵ* (see Syr ad loc.), aphel of *mlk*, meaning 'he became king' (Heb. *mālaḵ*). The 'Hebrew' word *hmlk* is therefore to be vocalized *himlīḵ*, or better (in view of the absence of a vowel letter to indicate a long *ī*) simply, in Aramaic fashion, *hamliḵ* (cf. the plurals in 5:29; 6:7, 12, 16). This is on a par with *tinten* (8:12).[65] Both stem from a translator, not an author.

9. Dan 10:3: 'I ate no delicacies, neither came flesh nor wine into my mouth, neither did I anoint myself ... .' In the two spaces I have left blank the Authorized and Revised Versions have 'at all.' That is a very good rendering of the Hebrew cognate infinitive absolute, in this case *sōḵ*; but when one compares Deut 28:40 and Micah 6:15 (also Ezek 16:9 and Amos 6:6), one can not help wondering why the Hebrew has not the substantive *šemen* 'with oil' instead. Now let us look at the Peshitta to our passage and imagine that the Hebrew is not available. In the phrase *wmšḥ' l' mšḥt* one might vocalize the first word *wamšāḥā*, literally 'and anointing,' in which case the phrase would mean 'neither did I anoint myself at all' (Hebrew *wsōḵ lō sāḵtī*). But if one had the presence of mind to look up what corresponds to the Syriac *mšḥ'* in the aforementioned parallel passages, one would end by confidently vocalizing the first word *wmešḥā* and rendering the phrase by 'neither did I anoint myself with oil,' Hebrew *wšemen lō sāḵtī*. Evidently, therefore, the Hebrew phrase of the MT goes back to an Aramaic original *wmšḥ*[66] *l' mšḥt*; whose first word was read *umšāḥ* (=Heb. *wsōḵ*) by the translator, but *umšaḥ* (with short *a*, =Heb. *wšemen*) by the author.

10. In 10:13 and 10:20 we have twice a puzzling 'I' where the context cries out for 'he.' In both cases the translator seems to have misread אנה 'I' for דנה 'this one, the latter.' In v. 13 the phrase may have been ודנה אתותר/אשתאר 'and the latter has remained,' the translator's mistake being facilitated by the fact that אתותר or אשתאר can be the first person singular imperfect

as well as the third person singular masculine perfect. In v. 20 ודנה נפק 'and when this one leaves' was mistaken for ואנה נפק 'and when I leave.'

11. In 11:4 the use of the verb *ḥṣy* in the sense of 'to divide (into *more than two* parts)' is unexampled except for Jud 7:16; 9:43, where it has a special military sense. Our *tēḥāṣ* is no more an imitation of these eleventh century models than the *ya'modnā* of 8:22 is of a tenth century model.[67] It is simply the result of the following proportion: *plaḡ* (7:25) : *ḥṣī* (12:7) :: *titpleḡ* (cf. 2:41) : x. Because the translator at least knew better than to employ the verb *ḥāṣā* in the sense of 'to distribute,' he rendered *yip̄loḡ* correctly by *yḥalleq* in 11:39.

12. As Bevan (p. xii) points out, we have in 11:17bα the Syriac idiom *yaḇ bneššē* 'to give in marriage.' The Aramaic was probably something like this וברתה בנשין ינתן לה לחבלותה 'and his daughter shall he give unto him in marriage in order to destroy him.'[68] The translator took the pronominal suffix of לחבלותה as feminine instead of masculine, and probably rendered the first two words by ובתו בנשים, of which our reading is a corruption. The entire clause ought to have been rendered something like this: ואת בתו יתן לו לאשה להאבידו.

13. *Ušnēhem hammlāḵīm* (v. 27) is a literal rendering of an Aramaic *utrēhōn malḵayyā* (cf. Syr) 'and both kings.' It is very unHebrew, and would hardly have occurred in a document composed (even by an Aramaic speaker) in Hebrew.

ADDENDA TO SECTION IV

1. To p. 27 below.

The resemblance to the Ahikar story was pointed out by G. A. Barton in *The American journal of Semitic languages and literatures* 16 (1899/1900): 242 ff., years before the discovery of the famous Aramaic Ahikar papyri of the fifth century B. C. E. at Elephantine; whose readers were almost certainly the Jewish community of that island, since all the non-literary Aramaic writings found there concern Jews.

2. To pp. 29–38.

From the identities of the three kings of Dan 7:24b (*Ba*), it follows that the stratum Bd-*Ba* Bb^d-*Bc* presupposes Epiphanes' brilliant victory over Artaxias of Armenia (see p. 22, top) in the second half of 165 B. C. E. (W. Otto, *Zur geschichte der zeit des 6. Ptolemäers* = Abhandlungen der Bayerischen Akademie der Wissenschaften, Phil.-hist. Abt. NF 11, 1934, pp. 85–86). Yet it is free from any trace of the king's amnesty and the end of the religious persecution in the winter of 164 (see p. 20, below). Its formation therefore falls between these surprisingly close termini. The next youngest layer, Bc-Bb^c, reflects a situation prior to Epiphanes' expedition to the East, since it anticipates instead a third Egyptian campaign (11:40 ff.), and was therefore deposited before the summer of 165. The mood and content of its immediate predecessor, Bb, seem to suit best a date not too long after the desecration of the temple ca. December 167; while Ba, we have seen, antedates this event, and may have come into being in the second half of the year 168 or even earlier (p. 29 f.).

NOTES

NOTES TO SECTION I

[1] In *KKLK*.

[2] The Hebrew portions of Daniel are translated from Aramaic originals; see below, Section V.

[3] 'A year later,' or 'in the following year,' makes excellent sense. Epiphanes' two expeditions to Egypt took place in two successive years: 169 and 168.

[4] For early examples, see Liddell and Scott, *A Greek-English lexicon*, ed. 1940; p. 2008b; for later ages, E. A. Sophocles, *Greek lexicon of the Roman and Byzantine periods*, 1888: p. 1173a; in modern Greek **χρόνος** is the regular word for 'year.'

[5] See *Journal of biblical literature* 56 (1937): 142 f.

[5a] [There is an eighth in 5:20.]

[6] The entire passage Dan 7:4–7 will be discussed fully in Section II.

[7] Charles, Montgomery, and Bentzen ad loc.; B.-L., para. 285; Torrey 1946: 11 b with n. 20.

[8] If the Masoretes had taken *hqmt* (v. 5) as a passive, they would have vocalized it as a normal passive: *h°qāmaṯ*, since its spelling would not have necessitated inventing a monstrosity like *h°qīmaṯ* as a compromise. Moreover, since all mss. have הֳקִימַת in v. 4, an original הֲקָמַת in v. 5 can easily have become contaminated by it, but an original הֳקָמַת in v. 5 would have been unlikely to become differentiated from it.

[9] Prof. S. Lieberman informs me that in the Palestinian Talmud the masc. and fem. pl. perf. usually end in *-wn* and *-yn* respectively (cf. Syriac *qṭalūn* and *qṭalēn*), and that irregularities are doubtless due to the graphic similarity of the two endings in the Hebrew script.

[10] See T. Nöldeke, *Beiträge zur semitischen sprachwissenschaft*, 1904, p. 20.— With Aramaic *qṭálū*, perfect, 3rd pers. pl. *masc.* — *qṭálī*, perfect, 3rd pers. pl. *fem.*, cf. Accad. *šū* 'he,' *šī* 'she'; *šunu* 'they' (m.), *šina* 'they' (f.). See C. Brockelmann, *Grundriss der vergleichenden grammatik der semitischen sprachen* I, 1908, para. 104 f-g.

[11] In most cases the result is likewise a substitution of masc. pl. for fem. pl., namely of the pronominal suffix *-hōn* for *-hēn*. A qre generally restores the correct suffix; not, however, in 7:12, where read *šolṭānhēn* and *lhēn*.

NOTES TO SECTION II

[*] This Section owes much to the admirable historical erudition and judgment of Prof. Elias J. Bickerman, upon which I have been able to draw not only thru the publications so frequently cited herein but also by personal contact.

[1] By Joseph Ward Swain, 'The theory of the four monarchies, opposition history under the Roman Empire,' *Classical philology* 35 (1940): 1–21. — In *Basler*

zeitschr. f. gesch. u. altertumskunde 42 (1943): 56 n. 47, which I have not seen, H. Fuchs furnishes some additional data (according to W. Baumgartner, *Theol. zeitschr., Basel,* 1 [1945]: 17 n. 3).

[2] Inasmuch as we shall have repeated occasion to point out that the book of Daniel's view of history was based as much upon prophecy as upon history, it is worth noting that nowhere in prophetic literature is there anything on Assyria to compare with the amazing doctrine of Jer 27:5 ff. that the Maker of the earth and of man and beast had designated Nebuchadnezzar, the king of Babylon, and his son and his son's son after him, to rule them all (cf. Dan 2:38). For even to Isaiah, 'Asshur' (not even any particular king of Assyria) is but the rod of YHWH's anger (Isa 10:5–6); not, so to speak, His vicar upon earth for any prescribed period of time. To be sure, if Judah tries to outwit YHWH and break His rod, she will only be beaten all the harder; but if she submits unconditionally to YHWH He will remove the rod Himself (most clearly Isa 30:15–16). Assyrian domination is not inevitable per se, still less has its duration been determined in advance.

[3] The error was therefore not exclusively, perhaps not even primarily, due to the existence of prophecies which seemed to predict the conquest of Babylon by the Medes rather than the Persians (against Charles, p. 141). But the prophecies in question were undoubtedly a contributing factor: cf. below n. 34. — Of course there still remains to be explained the figure of 'Darius the Mede' as the representative of Median power in this succession. The most widely accepted explanation is that it originated in some confused recollection of the *re*capture of rebellious Babylon in 520 by Darius I Hystaspis; who of course was not a Mede but a Persian, and the second successor rather than a predecessor of Cyrus. See Rowley *DM*, 54–60.

[4] V. 1a may be an Epiphanian interpolation. For while Daniel A (chs. 1–6) notes the two terminal dates of Daniel's public life in the first and last verses respectively of the introductory ch. 1, ch. 2 is the only one of the intervening episodes to be furnished with a date. When, therefore, it is observed that each of the four apocalypses in Daniel B (chs. 7–12) — namely, chs. 7, 8, 9 and 10–12 — is dated, obviously for the purpose of inspiring, by circumstantial details, confidence in the genuineness of these long-term predictions, and when it is further noted that ch. 2 likewise contains a prediction of events to be fulfilled in the reader's time (unlike chs. 4 and 5, whose predictions were fulfilled in Daniel's own lifetime), the hypothesis that its date was added at the time when Daniel B was appended to Daniel A becomes possible tho not necessary. (In any case, the motive for furnishing it with a date is, as just noted, to authenticate a still unfulfilled prediction; and since no such motive is present in the other chapters of Daniel A, these were originally undated as in MT, their dating in LXX being — as so much else in the LXX version of Daniel is by most scholars acknowledged to be — pure midrash.)

[5] After saying so explicitly in 1926, Baumgartner in 1939 adopted the view that only the content of chs. 1–6 antedates the second century C.E., whereas its literary fixation was undertaken in the reign of Epiphanes and for the express purpose of comforting the Jews who were faithful to their religion; so that the

secondary elements in ch. 2 are a fortiori Epiphanian. (See W. Baumgartner, *BD* 18 and *DF* 75–77.) In the light of the following argumentation, especially the unassailable interpretation of Dan 2:44, Baumgartner's change of front was indubitably a retrograde step; but I was guilty of the same deplorable retrogression in the *Louis Ginzberg jubilee volume* (English section), 1945: 165 n. 19, as against *KKLK* (1940): 74. I fell into this error because of a reluctance to admit that certain features of the Aramaic of Daniel were already widely current in the third century B.C.E. The reluctance was evidently warranted in the case of the feature which caused me the most misgivings, namely that of the alleged substitution of masculine for feminine forms of the third person plural perfect; but I have now proved (Section I B 2) that as a matter of fact no such substitution takes place in the Aramaic of Daniel. And whatever the causes of my aberration, an aberration it was.

In passing I would correct an error that has crept into Baumgartner's reporting (*DF* 76) of the views of recent Continental writers on the subject. Eissfeldt, para. 6, pp. 580–1, clearly sees 'in c. (1) 2:4b — 6 ein älteres aramäisches buch'; and Bentzen only points out how the tales, already existing *as literature*, acquired new meaning for Epiphanian readers (e. g. p. 11 below; p. 21, ll. 11 ff.).

[6] Vocalize *molḵayyā*; cf. *malḵū*(*ṯā*), vv. 39, 40, 41, 42; see *KKLK* (cf. Section I, before note 1); and below, before n. 12.

[7] In v. 4 the phrase 'it was taken away from the earth' can have only one meaning: 'it perished.' Non-Jewish apocalyptists employ the identical phrase in predicting the destruction of Rome. See Lactantius, *Divinae institutiones* VII, 15:11 (tolletur e terra), 19 (sublatu iri ex orbe); *Sibylline oracles* VIII, 39. (These three passages are quoted, though not in the present context, by H. Fuchs, *Der geistige widerstand gegen Rom in der antiken welt*, and by Swain, op. cit. [see above, n. 1]). Cf. also the phrase 'to perish from the earth' in biblical Aramaic (Jer 10:11) and Hebrew (Job 18:17) and the post-biblical *he'ḇīr min hā'āreṣ* 'to cause to pass away from the earth' ('Alenu prayer and High Holyday addition to the third bendiction of the 'Amidah), also *nōṭēl ḥayyāw min hā'ōlām* 'he destroys himself' (Mishnah Abot 4) and *moṣī'īn 'eṯ hā'āḏām min hā'ōlām* 'they destroy one' (ibid. 2, 3, 4). Note that the cited line in the *Sibylline oracles* — κἀξεδαφισθήσῃ καὶ πῦρ σὲ ὅλην δαπανήσει 'yea, thou wilt be taken away from the earth, and fire will consume thee entire' — combines the expression employed in v. 4 with reference to the fate of the first beast with that employed in v. 12b with reference to the fate of the fourth. Moreover, the phrase *ḥāzē hwēṯ*/*hwaiṯā 'aḏ dī* 'as I (thou) looked(est) on' always introduces an annihilation; see 2:34 f.; 7:9 ff. (As can be seen by comparing these two passages, the secondary link between 7:11b and the likewise secondary v. 8 (see further on) does not consist simply of v. 11a but of 11a minus the word *bēḏain* plus the first *four* words of 11b, cf. below n. 40). — As for the conclusion of v. 4, its incompatibility with the previous annihilation of the beast is only one of many indications that it is out of place. Another will be pointed out in n. 24, and the rest in due course.

[7a] Which had been without a kingdom since 587 B.C.E.

[8] In 7:17 too, the vocalization intended by the author is *molḵīn*; cf. *malḵū*(*ṯā*)/*malḵwaṯa*, vv. 23, 24 (cf. above n. 6).

[9] Not even the latest writer, Michael J. Gruenthaner, 'The four empires of Daniel,' *The Catholic biblical quarterly* 8 (1946): 78–82, 201–212. Gruenthaner does observe on p. 79 that Dan 2:34–35, 44 implies that 'the four (*recte*, the first three) kingdoms will survive in some form even after the period of their dominance is ended.' But on p. 72 we read: '. . . the first and second have already disappeared when the fourth arises' (true, but because they are thereupon reconstituted — see below — their temporary disappearance is disregarded by the biblical author); and on p. 81 he blinks the only interpretation of 7:12 which is compatible with the context, namely that the Median and Persian *kingdoms* (see above, n. 8) will survive the loss of empire.

[10] Ἡ Ἀτροπάτιος Μηδία, so named for Atropates, the founder of its dynasty; Strabo, *Geography* XI, 13:1; cf. τὴν Ἀτροπατίαν Μηδίαν, ibid. 5:6.

[10a] Strabo, ibid., XV, 3:24; cf. 3:3. — The dynasts of Persis (who may have claimed to be Achaemenids) achieved sufficient autonomy to coin currency of their own not later than about 280 B.C.E.; cf. E. T. Newell, *The coinage of the eastern Seleucid mints* 1938: 159–161. They had been let pretty much alone since about 300; E. E. Herzfeld, *Archaeological history of Iran* (The Schweich Lectures of the British Academy 1934), London 1935, p. 46.

[10b] Bickerman *NHPC*, 75.

[11] Bickerman *IS*, 22.

[12] Read once again *molḵīn*; see *KKLK* (cf. above, nn. 6 and 8).

[13] It is tempting to narrow the choice down to the second co-regency, that of Antiochus I's son Seleucus, in the years 279–268. For it ended with his father ordering him executed on a charge of high treason, which numismatists find borne out by the coins he struck in his own name; Bickerman *IS*, 219. During those years, therefore, there was particularly good reason for speaking of Babylonia as a kingdom. But there was also good enough reason during the preceding and following co-regencies.

[14] When the text says that the fourth kingdom will be divided, it means just that. It does not mean that it will rule over many nations. The latter was also true of each of the other kingdoms during its dominance, else it wouldn't have been a dominance. The writer is at pains to emphasize the universality of Babylonian rule (vv. 37–38): yet he never uses the expression 'divided' in connection with the Babylonian kingdom, neither does he call attention to the motley character of its subjects by representing it by more than one substance. Had he wanted to do that, he would have had to represent every one of the kingdoms not by two but by an unwieldy number of substances. Besides, our author distinguishes in the fourth monarchy not only two substances but two phases, the first of which he represents by iron alone. This imagery *could* very plausibly *be* interpreted to mean that the fourth kingdom would at first be all-powerful but later develop weakness. But to claim with Montgomery and Gruenthaner that that is how it *is* interpreted in v. 41a is something else again. *Malḵū p̄līḡā* means 'a divided kingdom' and nothing else, and its only possible implication is that the united Macedonian kingdom of Alexander will be divided between two royal lines — both of them purely Macedonian, of course. We know that there were actually more than two, but naturally enough the persons and territories of, for example,

Lysimachus and Cassander and their successors are of no interest to our author.

However, the Montgomery-Gruenthaner interpretation may very well have figured in an older tale which may have been adapted in Dan 2. There may also have been a still earlier version in which the feet as well as the legs were of pure iron, and in which the interpretation said nothing at all either about the division or about the decline of the fourth monarchy; but it is equally possible that the modification in the four-metal sequence was made prior to or simultaneously with its elaboration into a statue. For 'the iron image with the feet of clay' probably suggested to its creator just what it does to us. In any case, the possibilities envisaged in this paragraph are probable for (hypothetical) literary and oral *forerunners* of Dan 2, but not, as some Continental scholars believe, for earlier texts of Dan 2 itself. The latter, we have seen, was composed not earlier than 292 B.C.E., when the division of the Macedonian kingdom had already taken place. Since, therefore, the iron-and-tiling feet are not introduced (like the toes and the attempted fusion of the iron with the tiling) as an afterthought, v. 33 as it stands and v. 41a minus 'and the toes' were in all probability present in the text from the beginning.

[15] See Torrey 1909: 247–8. (I have substituted for Torrey's dates the slightly divergent ones which historians now assign to the events in question).

[16] Bickerman *NHPC*, 83.

[17] As for the reign of Antiochus IV Epiphanes, the Hellenizers among his Jewish subjects were too lacking in enthusiasm, for either the orthopraxy which Daniel and his companions exemplified or the kingdom of God whose coming Daniel predicted, to have had any share in the composition and transmission of this book; while others would not have expatiated upon the Greek kingdom's disunity, its attempts at consolidation, and the relative strength of its parts, while keeping mum about its wickedness. Cf. below, n. 21 — and contrast ch. 7!

[18] Not, however, by Eissfeldt.

[19] To be exact, it is only stated specifically in the case of the Macedonian kingdom. But the unmistakable implication of vv. 11–12 is that it had similarly been in consequence of a judgment by a divine tribunal that the second and third beasts had been stripped of their dominion but suffered to live, and hence the fate of the first beast must also have been determined in this way.

[20] On v. 4 see above, n. 7.

[21] The exegesis which discovers in the Nebuchadnezzar of Daniel a disguised Antiochus Epiphanes, and in what is related about him, especially in this chapter, a polemic against the Seleucid persecutor, is for cabalists. (It is even capable of identifying Darius with Antiochus in 6:15–29!) Cf. also above, n. 17.

[22] Only at one point has the vessel, instead, been adapted to the new content, namely in v. 33. The fourth kingdom is not represented by iron alone, but two phases are distinguished: a first represented by iron alone and a second represented by iron-and-tiling; the reason being that, as explained in vv. 40–41a, the initial unity of the kingdom would be followed by a cleavage. It is obviously by a further modification of this, already modified, scheme that the Parsee four-metal series — gold, silver, steel, and iron mixed with earth — arose. See J.

Scheftelowitz, *Die altpersische religion u. d. Jdtm.*, 1920: 220–228 (cited by Montgomery); Idem, *Zeitschr. f. missionskunde und religionswissenschaft* 42 (1927): 28 ff.

[23] As pointed out by Hölscher, p. 120.

The interpolator happens to have preferred the older word. For *'lū* also occurs in Daniel A (2:31; 4:7, 10) and is probably closely related to *hlw* of *CIS* ii 137, A 1, B 4; *NSI*, 202; whereas *'rū* is doubtless closely related to the *'rūm* of Palestinian targums, and more remotely to the *'rē* (=talmudic Hebrew *hrē* 'behold') of other targums, even tho these words are employed not as interjections but for rendering the Heb. *kī*, and that not only in the sense of (the conjunction) 'for' but also in those of 'if' and 'when.'

[23a] Cf. Section I B 1 on the abnormal vocalization of *slqt*.

[23b] No doubt because the Hebrew for this is *'ēnaim rāmōt*, literally 'lofty eyes.' A perfect commentary on the eleventh horn's mouth and eyes is 2 Ki 19:22//Isa 37:23.

[24] That such is its signification — Hölscher's phrase 'die überlegenheit über das tierische' is not specific enough — in v. 13 is vouched for by vv. 18, 21–22, 25, 27. As for v. 4, the impossibility of a pious Jew in his right mind having ascribed holiness to the Chaldean kingdom is only another proof (cf. above n. 7) that the last two clauses of this verse are out of place. It will not be long now before we find out where they belong.

[25] Above nn. 7 and 9.

[26] And not (*pace* Haller, Noth, Baumgartner *DF*) because he is writing between 333 and 323 B.C.E. and has not had time to become acquainted with the specific characteristics of the Macedonian monarchy. As for his silence about the fourth kingdom's divided state, he has no reason to mention it. For one thing, it was already mentioned in ch. 2, and our apocalyptist is merely supplementing chs. 1–6; and for another, it has not half the interest for him that it had for the author of ch. 2. Firstly, because what was still something of a novelty in the first half of the third century was no longer novel in the second century. And secondly, because when ch. 2 was written the Ptolemies could not be ignored because they ruled Judea, nor the Seleucids because they were even more powerful; whereas in the time of our author of ch. 7, which was the reign of Antiochus Epiphanes (175–163), that monarch not only ruled Judea, but in 169 (and 168) crushingly defeated his southern rival(s) Ptolemy VI (and VII) and donned the crown of Egypt. It is therefore not the case that in ch. 7 the fourth kingdom does *not yet* figure as a divided kingdom, but rather that divisions other than the Seleucid are *no longer* taken into consideration: no more than in the choice, in ch. 8, of the he-goat (i. e., **'Αἰγόκερως**, the sign of the zodiac Capricornus, governing Syria — see all recent commentaries) to represent 'the kingdoms of Greece' as a whole (8:21–23, on which see Section IV n. 16). Nor is the absence of any hint at weakness in the fourth kingdom in ch. 7 a sign of antiquity. On the contrary, just Epiphanes, at least until 165 B.C.E., was as little likely to impress the Jews as 'weak' as was Hitler in his heyday.

Since, therefore, our author means specifically the Seleucidae by the fourth monarchy there is even geographical and historical justification, which he may have had in mind, for his representing it as a reincarnation of the defunct Babylonian kingdom: Babylonia was not only a part of their realm but the original kingdom of Seleucus I. However, it is not suggested that he wouldn't have made the identification anyway; cf. the later identification of Rome with Babylon, Revelation 14:8, and Billerbeck, *Kommentar zum Neuen Testament aus Talmud und Midrasch* III, 1926, p. 816. (Finding more anti-Edomite than anti-Babylonian texts in the Scriptures, and attracted by the piquanterie of twin brothers as antitheses, the Rabbis more often stressed Rome's *Edomite* origin.)

[27] The claws are probably to be restored in v. 7 (with Baumgartner *BHK*[3]) from v. 19.

[28] Various commentators, beginning with certain authorities cited anonymously in Pseudo-Saadiah, have realized that that is the sense demanded by the context, but have been unable to offer a convincing etymological justification for it. I hardly doubt but the reading *wtlt ʿlʿyn* has arisen, thru a combination of haplography, dittography, and misreading of a common word for an unusual one, from an original *wtlt tlʿn*; **tlʿn* — perhaps vocalized **tālʿān* — being an Aramaic etymon of Hebrew *mṯallʿōṯ* 'fangs.' The form of the Hebrew word (and the suggested form of its conjectured Aramaic etymon) is that of a feminine plural participle (agreeing with *šinnaim* [*šinnain*] understood, like *ṭōḥnōṯ*, Koh 12:3) of a verb *tlʿ* 'to rend (flesh)'; from which, significantly, a finite form occurs only in an Aramaic text: Pseudo-Jonathan to Lev 1:17.

[29] At Bear Mountain, New York, a four-acre bear-pit was shared by a she-bear, her two cubs, and two adult males. When the whelps were a few months old, the wily keepers kidnapped them, one at a time, while the big bears' attention was engaged by food. After each loss the enraged mother administered an undeserved thrashing to her hapless companions. (After *The New York Times*, April 30, 1947, p. 27.)

[30] In nn. 2–3.

[31] See above, n. 7, end.

[32] See above, n. 24.

[33] Ibid.

[34] It is hardly necessary to point out that what matters in the present context is what *our* author inferred from those prophetic passages, not what *their* authors intended by them, nor what actually happened. Actually, it was not the Medes but the Persians who overthrew Babylon, and the prophetic passages cited may, like Greek and Minean sources of the Persian period, have employed the name 'Medes' in the sense of 'Persians.' But once the notion that the Medes were the successors of the Chaldeans had arisen in the manner explained at the beginning of this Section, it was inevitable that the name 'Medes' in those passages should be understood in its primary sense.

[35] At this point the reasonable reader will concede the necessity of rearranging vv. 4–5 as proposed, but would appreciate suggestions for even a partial explanation of the present disorder. If I am not mistaken, the person responsible for it (a) misinterpreted the 'raising from the earth' in v. 4 in the same way as many moderns ('elevation') and, (b) having our corrupt reading 'ribs' instead of 'fangs,' thought the 'three ribs' were part of the 'one side' of v. 5, which he

wrongly understood to refer to a side of beef or the like picked up by the second beast (if he is to be credited with that much reflection). For his probable identity, see below: n. 51, the end of this Section, and Section IV.

[36] The great sea is doubtless the great ocean (Heb. *thōm rabbā*, Gen 7:11; Isa 51:10; Amos 7:4; Ps 36:7) that lies around and beneath the earth, and is in every sense the opposite pole of heaven; see, e. g., Gen 7:11; 8:2; 49:25//Deut 33:13; Exod 20:4//Deut 5:8. The respective characters of the first four kingdoms on the one hand and the fifth on the other can therefore be inferred from the fact that the former are represented in the dream as emerging from the great ocean and the latter (v. 13) as arriving with the clouds of heaven. That the former appear as beasts and the latter as a human being signifies the same thing. Why the former are produced by the impact of the four winds of heaven upon the great ocean is not quite clear: probably just because the heathen kingdoms happened to be four in number they were conceived of as in some vague way representing each one of the cardinal points of the compass. The Babylonian kingdom might not improperly be said to have originated in the south, the Median in the north, the Persian in the east (it was known that in the days of its greatness its real center had been Susa in Elam—Neh 1:1; cf. Dan 8:2—not Persepolis-Istakhr in Persis, which is south as well as east of Babylonia) and the Greek in the west (cf. Dan 8:5, 21). That the beasts are not mythological survivals but transparent allegories is clear from the historiosophic and structural considerations in the foregoing discussion and will be clinched later on, when their numbered members will also be explained allegorically.

[37] Meaning perhaps one shoulder, as if to strike with its fore paw. Or alternatively one end, namely its forward end, for the purpose of assuming an erect posture; cf. the continuation in the text.

[37a] That the eleventh horn, tho it quickly grew to a greater size than its fellows (v. 20 end), was little at the moment when it sprouted goes without saying. That it is specially called 'a little one' is therefore due solely to the fact that it is borrowed from 8:9–12. There the horn described as 'little' actually is, and remains, smaller — at least in girth — than the five earlier horns of the he-goat (8:5, 8); since the latter represent kingdoms, whereas the little horn that branches off from one of them represents only a king of one of the kingdoms. (See Section V A.) In ch. 7, on the other hand, all of the horns represent kings, and the eleventh one represents a king actually greater than the others (v. 20 end, and v. 24b; in the latter perhaps read — cf. Th — *yiśgē* 'will be greater'). The attribute 'little' is therefore only mechanically borrowed from ch. 8, and a telling proof of the secondary character of all references to an eleventh horn in ch. 7.

[38] Anent the supposed foreign, or mythological, origins of this imagery, see the refreshing remarks of Montgomery, pp. 85 f., 297 f. After all, our author's heritage included Isa 41:4; 43:10; 48:3; Ps 90:1–2 among other things, and it is as the God of history that the Supreme Being acts here; ideas of which the imagery chosen is a very natural rendering in the language of apocalyptic vision. So while it *may* be borrowed in whole or in part, the way in which one bit after another of alleged mythology in this chapter has vanished into thin air upon

examination places the burden of proof — real proof — upon those who claim that it is.

38a Pure fleece, like white snow, never has been soiled; not even before it was shorn, since the sheep was made to wear a jacket. See Mishnah Nega'im 1:1 and TB Shabbat 54a. (I owe this observation to Prof. Saul Lieberman.)

39 Namely, the one for which the thrones (plural) of v. 9 had been set. It is the Celestial Tribunal, the *bēṯ-dīn šellma'lān* of the Rabbis (e. g. TP Rosh ha-Shanah II 58b), which includes associate judges.

40 As in 2:34 so in 7:9, the divine intervention is expressed by 'as I (thou) looked(est) on'; and as in 2:35 so in 7:11, the destruction of the heathen power(s) resulting from that intervention is introduced by 'then' (*bēḏain*). Cf. above, n. 7 near end.

41 I. e., the second and the third, the first having been annihilated long ago (v. 4); as we have explained repeatedly.

42 The suffix should be *-hēn*; see Section I B 2, with n. 11.

43 The Aramaic has no special forms for the past perfect, but one who translates into English has no excuse for not using this tense when the sense calls for it.

44 Cf. above, note 36. The manlike figure is as unmythological as the preceding beastlike ones.

45 Literally, 'within its sheath,' vocalizing *bḡō nḏānāh*; cf. TB Sanhedrin 108a; Genesis rabbah 26:6 (cited — and wrongly minimized — by Driver ad loc.). Further emendation — cf. Baumgartner *BHK*[3] ad loc. — is contra-indicated.

46 See above, n. 8.

46a '*The* saints of the Most High' would have been *qaddīšē 'elyōnayyā*; but this, like the simple *qaddīšayyā* ('the saints') is consistently avoided. There is no reason why this coyness should be lost in an English translation.

47 See Baumgartner *BHK*[3] ad loc.

47a Literally 'visibility,' or 'conspicuousness'; cf. Section V n. 29. For 'appearance' the author would probably have said *rēw* (see 2:31b). I think *ḥzōṯeh* — again literally 'its visibility' — said with reference to a tree in 4:8, 17, likewise means 'its thickness.' That some such meaning seems to be required there by the context has been felt before, as can be seen from the note of Baumgartner *BHK*[3] on 4:8. — Of course 7:20b does not contradict 7:8. Once the 'little' horn had 'sprouted up' it was no longer little, witness the three others that were uprooted before it; cf. 8:9 and see above, n. 37a.

48 See n. 46a.

48a Cf. Baumgartner *BHK*[3] ad loc.

48b That these lines are intended to be metrical in the original Aramaic is far from certain. At any rate, the interpretative verses belonging to the primary stratum (Roman type in the translation) resist all attempts at scansion, despite Montgomery's rendering of all of vv. 23–27 in stichs consisting of two hemistichs each.

49 On *'iddān* 'year' see Section I A.

50 Namely 'that kingdom's,' v. 24a. Vocalize *šolṭānāh*, making the pronominal suffix agree with *malḵūṯā* in v. 24a; for vv. 24b–25 are the work of the second apocalyptist.

[51] But as we shall see at the end of this Section, even this was not understood quite correctly by the second apocalyptist, so most likely he did not understand the meanings of the unexplained numbers at all. Not improbably, therefore, it was he who jumbled vv. 4–5. Whether or not it was he, and whether or not the motives for the operation were those suggested above in n. 35, it was tantamount to (unwittingly) springing a combination lock on a burglar-proof box containing the key to the unexplained numbers. The combination, as we have seen, is 4a, 5aγ-b, 4ba-β, 5aα-β, 4bγ-δ.

[52] See the editor's note to Seder 'olam rabbah XXIX ed. Ratner, p. 134. — By the way, is it likely that a person writing less than a decade after the death of Darius III would have gone quite so far astray? — another disturbing thought for those who date Dan 7 in the reign of Alexander.

[53] E. g., Seder 'olam rabbah, ibid. p. 136 f. (see the manuscript readings cited by the editor). From Ezr 6:14 the Rabbis inferred that Darius the Persian was also called Cyrus and Artaxerxes (see TB Rosh ha-shanah 3b and Tosafot ad loc.), but their further inference that *all* the Achaemenian kings assumed the throne-name of Artaxerxes was, as Prof. Bickerman illuminatingly suggests (orally), inspired by the practice of the Arsacid kings, with which they were naturally familiar, of calling themselves Arsaces.

[54] It may be that 'Ahasuerus' as the name of Darius the Mede's father (9:1) stands for 'Cyaxares' (the case for this identification is best stated by C. C. Torrey, 1946: 7b–8a), and it may also be that Cyaxares was known to have been a king. But the characteristic numbers of our beasts are concerned exclusively with princes who exercised *imperial* sway; see below, n. 57.

[55] That the expression *wlšṭr ḥd hqmt* (v. 5) must mean 'and it raised up one ruler' was sensed by Leroy Waterman, *Journal of biblical literature* 65 (1946): 59–61. But it does not mean that (or anything else) in Hebrew, and neither does it mean it literally. In none of the four cases is the number of sovereigns indicated by a literal gloss, but only by some peculiarity in the anatomy, or — as apparently in this case — in the stance, of the dream-beast.

[56] See reference above, n. 53.

A Jewish chronology with three Median and five Persian kings, such as that reconstructed by Torrey 1946, never existed. The rabbinical texts he cites are partly corrupt (which is why in some cases I refer specifically to the *manuscript* readings in Seder 'olam rabbah) and partly misunderstood. The one from TB Rosh ha-Shanah 3b is badly misunderstood (see above, n. 53). The one from the Second Targum on Esther 1:1 is both misunderstood and corrupt. The textus receptus reads 'Ahasuerus the Persian (nota bene!), the son of Darius the Mede'; and even if this were correct it could not possibly imply that 'Ahasuerus the Persian' was a Mede (!), but would only represent a late midrashic combination which, having in mind the widespread practice of papponymy, made Ahasuerus a son of Darius the Mede because he bore the same name as the latter's father (Dan 9:1). But the reading of the textus receptus obviously is not original but has evolved, thru the loss of the words בר כורש (partly owing to homoeoteleuton: אחשורוש בר כורש פרסאה), from the reading in the edition of M. David, *Das Targum scheni u. s. w.*; which, representing the consensus of three manuscripts, goes like this: 'Ahasuerus (=Xerxes) the son of Cyrus the Persian the son of Darius the Mede.' Quite naturally, the supposed second of the Medo-Persian monarchs was made a son of the supposed first, and the supposed third a son of the supposed second. — That the biblical underpinning of Torrey's structure is not very firm either may also be illustrated by a single example. That Dan 6 and the book of Esther assume that the Medes and the Persians formed a coalition during the periods of their dominance is rightly inferred by Torrey (as already by the Babylonian amora Raba, TB Megillah 12a) from the former's repeated invocation of 'the laws of the Medes and Persians' and the latter's way of talking about 'the power of Persia and Media' (Esth 1:3), 'the seven princes of Persia and Media' (1:14), 'the princesses of Persia and Media' (1:18), 'the laws of the Persians and the Medes' (1:19), and 'the book of the chronicles of the kings of Media and Persia' (10:2). Torrey is also obviously right in attributing the order in which the two nations are named in Dan 6 to the fact that with 'Darius the Mede' on the throne the Medes were the senior partners. Nothing could be more natural than to account for the opposite order in Esth 1 by the corresponding circumstance that 'in those days . . . the (Persian) king Ahasuerus sat on the throne of his kingdom'; but Torrey finds in it merely a confirmation of Ahasuerus' Median (!) nationality: 'The Medo-Persian union is still standing, but it is now nearing its end. The Persian power has the upper hand, and is ready to take over the whole administration; Ahasuerus II [the first being the aforementioned father of Darius the Mede — H. L. G.] is the last of the Median emperors.' That in Esth 10:2 the order is again 'Media and Persia' is attributed by Torrey to a lack on the part of the redactor who appended ch. 10 of sufficient finesse to adapt himself to the style of the body of the book. That would be a plausible explanation, were there not a much better one; since the coalition's first ruler, or — if the coalition was believed to have existed before the reign of 'Darius the Mede' — its first rulers, was (were) a Mede (Medes) and the later ones Persians (cf. Dan 8:3bγ: Torrey's theory of alternations rests upon nothing), the joint *chronicles* must necessarily relate the events of the Median reign(s) before those of the Persian reigns.

57 E. g., in Seder 'olam rabbah ch. 28 (ed. Ratner, p. 126). In Canticles rabbah 3:3 and Esther rabbah 3, there is a legend which deserves to be cited not only for its beauty but in confirmation of the principle, which I have repeatedly stressed, that the history of a monarchy neither necessarily begins nor necessarily ends with its world hegemony. Of kings that reigned over Babylon before Nebuchadnezzar, the Bible has preserved the name of at least one, Merodachbaladan (2 Ki 20:12 // Isa 39:1), and in a pinch one could add Amraphel, the king of Shinar (Gen 14:1); but these were not, in the language of the Midrash, קוזמוקר/ל/טורין (*κοσμοκράτορες*). The legend I have referred to relates that Merodach-baladan, inquiring of his sages the reason for the abnormally long day of 2 Ki 20:11//Isa 38:8, was informed that it had all happened for the sake of Hezekiah, the king of Judah. He thereupon dispatched a message of 'Greeting to King Hezekiah, greeting to the city of Jerusalem, greeting to the great God.' As the messengers were departing, it was pointed out to him that 'the great God' ought to have been named first. So Merodach-baladan rose from his throne, advanced

three steps to call the messengers back, and had the letter rewritten. For walking three steps to honor God, he was rewarded by God with three descendants who were קוזמוקרטורין: Nebuchadnezzar, Evil-merodach, and Belshazzar. — See L. Ginzberg, *The legends of the Jews* IV, p. 275 f.; VI, 368 n. 83.

[58] And if I'm not mistaken, even he was anticipated by the original version of the mene-tekel story. See Section III.

[59] See P. Schnabel, *Berossos*, 1923, p. 5; cited by Baumgartner *DF*, 204.

[60] He was assassinated in 310/9; Bickerman *NHPC*, 75.

[61] So Baumgartner (see n. 59); who, however, because he errs with Hölscher, Haller, Noth, and Bentzen in connecting v. 7bβ with the secondary v. 8 instead of with the primary v. 7, does not realize that the ten horns include Antiochus Epiphanes, and is therefore compelled to include Antiochus the younger (son of Seleucus IV) in the series as the tenth. However, the case of Antiochus the younger is like that of Philip Arrhidaeus: he was co-monarch with Antiochus Epiphanes, but died before him; and moreover, he was more of a figurehead than either Philip Arrhidaeus or Alexander Aegus, whereas Epiphanes was a real king. If, therefore, Philip Arrhidaeus was not counted, what wonder if Antiochus the younger wasn't. See also n. 66.

[62] That an apocalyptist in the reign of Antiochus IV could not have known so much about the latter's predecessors will be argued by no one who remembers Dan 11 and knows its secrets.

[63] Hölscher, p. 120 f., points out that just the secondary parts of ch. 7 are strikingly akin to passages in ch. 8–12. That is because they likewise date from the time of the actual religious persecution. See Section IV.

[64] See, for example, Bickerman *GM*, 63–80; I Macc 1:10–40.

[65] Even if they were, perhaps, not yet so desperate as to take up arms against him from religious motives. Bickerman *GM*, pp. 68–70, stresses the purely political character of the rising of 168.

[66] For example, I expect all competent scholars to agree some day that no system is plausible which includes among the three kings whom Epiphanes humbled (literally, to be sure, 'laid low,' v. 24b) either Antiochus III or Seleucus IV, whose violent deaths were not his doing; or Demetrius, for whose exile he was likewise not to blame, and who moreover did not become a king until after Epiphanes' demise; or Heliodorus, who never became a king at all. As for Antiochus the younger, the Jewish apocalyptists — who were concerned with the heathen kingdoms and kings that would in fact 'arise' (vv. 17, 24) and not with pretenders, however 'legitimate' — would have said that Epiphanes 'raised him up' rather than 'laid him low' by recognizing him as joint king from 174 to 170 (Bickerman *IS*, 22), even if he did keep him in a subordinate position. However, he did lay him low if he was the instigator of his murder, as no doubt he was. But since the other kings that can — without artificiality — be said to have been humbled by Epiphanes (a) are kings in fact and not just in name, (b) are rulers of foreign nations, (c) are militarily defeated, not either relegated to obscurity by political maneuvering or assassinated, and (d) constitute a trio without the younger Antiochus, consistency rules the latter out from among the three uprooted horns. Plausibility, on the other hand, rules him out from among

the seven horns that are not uprooted before the upstart eleventh; for if he was counted at all he ought to have been added to those that were uprooted. Evidently, therefore, the second apocalyptist disregards him altogether, just like the first one (see above, n. 61). In its time, his introduction into the discussion of Dan 7 was warranted; today, his elimination is about due.

[67] So already Porphyry *apud* Jerome on Dan 7:8 (ed. Migne, col. 531) and E. F. C. Rosenmüller, *Scholia in Vetus Testamentum, pars decima Danielem continens*, Lipsiae 1832, p. 238 (both cited—but alas rejected—by Rowley *DM*, 108).

[67a] *Das buch Daniel*, 1894, p. 46.

[68] Cf. above, n. 37a, and below, Section IV n. 16.

NOTES TO SECTION III

[1] The pertinent literature is reviewed by E. G. Kraeling, The handwriting on the wall, *Journal of biblical literature* 63 (1944): 11–18.

[2] See *BHK*[3] to Dan 5:25.

[3] Op. cit.

[4] Op. cit., p. 18.

[5] See Section II near the end. — It is, by the way, very probable indeed that Jewish knowledge of the Chaldean dynasty was already limited to these three representatives by the time of, say, Nehemiah; and the version of the mene-tekel story in which the three weights were identified with these three figures may perfectly well have arisen in the Persian age.

[6] See Section II near the beginning.

[7] Heb. *'wīl* 'a fool.' The combination is fanciful to be sure. But neither the book of Daniel, nor ch. 5 thereof, nor even vv. 24–27 of ch. 5, are fancy-free. In Section II we pointed out some remarkable agreements between the reasoning of Dan 7 and the Midrash of the Rabbis as to how many Chaldean (and Median, and Persian) *kosmokratores* there were. It is therefore pertinent to recall here the following haggadah by Rabbi Tanḥuma (fourth century C.E.): Ahasuerus's incredible wealth (Esth 1:3–8) had been recovered by Cyrus from the bottom of the Euphrates. For Nebuchadnezzar, after gathering all the wealth in the world, had loaded it all onto copper ships and diverted the Euphrates from its course in order to cover them up. This Nebuchadnezzar had done because in his meanness he couldn't bear the thought of leaving that fortune to אויל (in the Esther rabbah version the second element of his 'son's' name, מרודך, is omitted, hardly by chance) — a thought obviously inspired by Koh 2:18–19. See Midrash Abba Gorion to Esth 1:4 and Esther rabbah to the same verse. [It is not quite clear whether the Euphrates was permanently diverted to a new course in order to cover the treasure or whether the treasure was deposited on the original bed and the river then turned back to that bed. The many parallels collected, without a knowledge of the rabbinical legend, by Alexander H. Krappe, Les funerailles d'Alaric, *Annuaire de l'Institut de philologie et d'histoire orientales et slaves* 17 (1939–44): 228–240, suggest the latter alternative. The closest parallel is from

Dio Cassius LXVIII, 14, 4. The others concern burials of unusual personalities under river beds rather than caches of treasure. I owe this reference to Prof. S. Lieberman.]

[8] In Tosefta Rosh ha-shanah 11 (1), 211, l. 10 (and parallels), a spiritually worthless person is called *qal šebbaqqallīm* 'levissimus.' The same passage cites Jerubbaal, Samson, and Jephthah as examples of 'ultra-light' leaders (*qallē 'ōlām*) and Moses, Aaron and Samuel as 'ultra-weighty' ones (*ḥmūrē 'ōlām*).

NOTES TO SECTION IV

[1] Everybody knows the parallel story of Joseph. Compare also, for example, the vizier Shammāsh at the court of Julai'ād in the Arabian Nights.

[2] See Bickerman *GM*, 12–13.

[3] Section II, n. 37a and text before n. 68.

[4] I shall select from among his examples those similarities which are in my opinion both real and characteristic.

[5] The form and meaning of this last expression will be discussed in Section V, A 2.

[6] In my opinion ישחית is not a corruption of ישיח but a rendering of an Aramaic יחבל; the latter, however, may be a corruption of ימלל. For the translation character of 1:1–2:4a and chs. 8–12, see Section V.

[7] For 'final phase' as the sense of *qēṣ* in Bc see further on.

[8] 12:4b is difficult. This is the best rendering I know.

[9] Vv. 11 and 12 are agreed to be two successive corrections of v. 7.

[10] See Section I A.

[11] That *mar'ē* came to be used in this sense thru translation from the Aramaic I shall endeavor to prove in Section V B. For proof that it does have some such sense here, the verb *ne'mar* 'was uttered' and a glance at vv. 13–14, from which it is clear that 'the *mar'ē* about morning and evening' is something that Daniel has heard (*wā'ešm'ā . . . mdabbēr . . . wayyōmer. . . hamdabbēr. . . wayyōmer*), not seen, may suffice for the present.

[12] Judge for yourself from this: (15) Now when I, Daniel, beheld the vision, *I sought understanding*. And behold, something like the image of a man was standing before me. (17) He came over to where I was standing, and when he came I was terrified and dropped on my face. Then he addressed me thus: '*Understand*, O son of man, for the vision relates to the time of the end.'

[13] V. 26b: But do thou keep the vision a secret, for it relates to a distant future.

[13a] See Section V C 4.

[14] The exact figure is more optimistic than the round one; but according to I Macc 1:54; 4:52–53, the temple service was actually restored in three years and 10 days. Assuming that no leap years intervened, that would make, since there are 354 days to a lunar year, only 1072 days or 2144 evenings and mornings. There is therefore no reason why the apocalyptist should not have expected this (and much else) to come about in 1150 days or 2300 evenings and mornings,

while calling this period 'half a septennium' in 9:27 for the sake of remaining within the scheme of septennia.

With every possible reservation, I should like to record the following thought. If, taking the 15th of Kislev, 145 Seleucid Era, Jewish style (I Macc 1:54), as the starting point and counting alternately 29 and 30 days to a lunar month (354 days to a lunar year), we could assume that the word ושלשים has dropped out by haplography after ושלש מאות in 8:14, the period of the persecution would last exactly thru the 29th of Addar, or the very last day, of 148 Sel., Jewish style (approximately vernal equinox 163). The apocalyptist may have assumed that the cycle of 70 weeks of years would end precisely with the calendar year 148 Sel., Jewish style, even tho the persecution had begun two and a half months later than the exact middle of the last septennium. — By the way, the year Tishri 148 Sel. — Elul 149 Sel. (autumnal equinox 164 — autumnal equinox 163) was a sabbatical year (Bickerman *GM* 14, 157), and the last supplementer, in 12:12, probably thought the cycle of weeks of years would only be completed with the whole of the sabbatical year.

[15] Even if Darius the Mede is assumed to have reigned only one year, three years elapsed between 9:1 and 10:1, and he actually had an expectancy of eight years of life at the time of his accession (Dan 6:1; cf. Ps 90:10).

[15a] That the purpose of this sentence is to make just this identification becomes even more apparent when one turns it back into its original Aramaic and discovers that it contains a play on the name Gabriel; as is done in Section V A 1, iii a, which see. — Dan 10:1b is probably also from the hand of Bd; see below, Section V n. 60.

[16] Hölscher's point (p. 128) that 'In 2:39; 7:5 f. Media and Persia are two empires, appearing successively and represented by two different symbols; in 8:3 f., 20 Medo-Persia is a single empire, represented by the two-horned ram' is ill taken. Hölscher himself (p. 121) rightly attributes to *mlky* in 8:20 the meaning of 'kingdoms' (and in accordance with *KKLK* we must vocalize here too *molḵē*); otherwise the implication would be that Media and Persia each produced only one emperor, an idea that is not to be imputed to any biblical author. And that the Persian monarchy was neither identical nor contemporaneous with the Median but posterior to it is expressed quite unambiguously in vv. 3b and 20b: the taller horn sprouts up after the shorter one, Persia is named after Media.

To be sure, Bb must have known that the Medes and Persians were kindred peoples and he probably believed that they formed a coalition (which is why he represented them by a single animal); but that is also the assumption of Daniel 6 and the Book of Esther, and Daniel A and Esther nevertheless assume that the Median and Persian *monarchies* were distinct and successive (see Section II, n. 56). If, therefore, Bb tells us as plainly as he can that he is of the same opinion, we have no right to think we know his mind better than he. Is it suggested that because he represented the closely related Greek kingdoms by one animal he did not, despite vv. 21–22, regard the kingdom of Alexander Magnus and Alexander Aegus and its four succession kingdoms as five distinct *kingdoms*? [In v. 21 read *molḵē* (final yod lost thru haplography) and *hammoleḵ*; for v. 22 proves beyond the shadow of doubt that the he-goat, like the ram, represents as many *kingdoms* as he has large horns, the first large horn of the goat being the *kingdom* of Alexander the Great and Alexander Aegus. Only a horn that branches off from one of the kingdom-horns represents a king, vv. 9–12, 23–25. — Correct *KKLK*, p. 73 ll. 9–10 from below, accordingly.]

17 Read *'ēḏ* in view of the parallelism and of Ps 27:12; Prov 6:19; 12:17; 14:5; 19:5, 9, and because prophetic texts were intended to convey an intelligible meaning. See also n. 19.

18 So rightly LXX. The masoretic pointing presupposes Dan Bc; see further on.

19 The texts cited in n. 17 and the observation that *yāpī/ē/ḥ* never occurs otherwise than as a parallel synonym of *'ēḏ* leave non-hairsplitters with no alternative to taking it as a substantive. — [In passing it may be remarked that there is no verb *pw/y/ḥ* in Cant 2:17; 4:6 either. For since the versions read the second verb in these passages ונסו the first is probably to be read שיפנה; cf. Jer 6:4. Elsewhere (Cant 4:16; Ps 10:5; 12:6; Ezek 21:36) the verb *pw/y/ḥ* may be retained.]

20 In 10:14b, in free quotation, *layyāmīm* 'for the days is substituted for *lammō'ēḏ*, thus confirming that in the remaining two passages *mō'ēḏ* means not 'fixed (future) *date*' but 'fixed (present) *period*.' (8:26bβ is different. In the absence of the word 'yet,' and with 'many days' instead of '*the* days,' this clause can only mean 'for it relates to a distant future'; cf. Ezek 12:27.)

21 They may be deliberate. Another bold reinterpretation of an old text by Bc was noted by me *apud* Bickerman *GM*, 170. Dan 11:30a imposes upon Num 24:24 the following sense: 'Ships shall come forth from Kittim (=the Romans)[a] and shall afflict Asshur (=the Seleucid Syrians),[b] who in turn shall afflict Eber (=the Hebrews.)'

[a]For כתים 'Romans' see LXX to Dan 11:30a, Targums to Num 24:24, and כיתין 'Rome' or 'Italy' in a Babylonian Aramaic incantation text of Jewish authorship (C. H. Gordon, *Archiv Orientální* 6 [1934]: 330).

[But be it noted that these Roman and Byzantine age identifications result from taking 'ships . . . from Kittim' as the subject of 'shall afflict' both times, since to the Jews after 63 B.C.E. the nation that came from overseas to afflict them and other Orientals could only be the Romans. And since Greek age Palestinians — other than our friend Bc — likewise construed Num 24:24 in this, more natural, way *they* necessarily identified Kittim with Macedonia; 1 Macc 1:1; 8:5.]

[b]The Prophets don't know this use of 'Asshur' for the simple reason that there is little of a Hellenistic date in the Prophets. It is an interesting fact that even Daniel Bc makes the identification only by such subtle allusions. Note how the language of Isa 8:8a is applied to the victorious sweep of Seleucid armies in Dan 11:10, 22, 26, 40, and how 11:36 identifies Epiphanes with the presumptuous rod of the Lord's anger which shall suffer condign punishment as soon as the Lord's anger with Israel has spent itself (Isa 10:5, 15, 23–26). [Similarly Alexander Balas is called 'the king of Canaan that dwelt in Assyria' in a retrojection of the battle of the plain of Antioch, at which Ptolemy VI was mortally wounded in 145 B.C.E., into the age of the Patriarchs, Jubilees 46:6, according to an oral comment of Prof. Bickerman.]

22 See above, nn. 17 and 19.

23 That *ḥāzōn* in 10:14 means not 'vision' but 'schedule of events' we learned but a while ago. In 11:14 the allusions are obscure. See most recently E. Taeubler, *The Jewish quarterly review* 37 (1946/7): 1–30, 125–137, 249–263. May *lha'mīḏ ḥāzōn* mean 'to cut the program short,' 'to halt the course of events'? (Or did the translator misread Aramaic להקמה חרו 'to establish liberty' as לי חזו?) — Bc's use of *ḥazōn* in the sense of 'schedule of events' is taken over by Bd at 9:24b.

24 But, like the man robed in linen of Bc, an anonymous one. I have shown above that 8:16 belongs not to Bb but to *Bb*, and is the work of the author of Bd.

25 This the writer Bd, whose revelation is of no less artificial a character, imitates (9:2–3, 21). Noth (p. 163) observes that chs. 10–12 contain not a vision but a discourse, but he fails to observe that that is just as true of ch. 9 (so already Bevan). 9:21 refers to ch. 8 as a vision (and wrongly includes the angel in it), but the experience of ch. 9 itself is called a 'word' and a 'revelation' (*mar'ē*), v. 23.

25a I shall have more to say about this *nirdam* in Section V C 7.

26 See above, n. 21[b].

27 The masoretic vocalization *lmō'ēḏ* leaves v. 19b without a subject. Theodotion, who interprets the consonants in the same way, borrows a subject from v. 17.

27a We noted above that he says *qaddīšē 'elyōnīn* where Bb (8:24) says *qḏōšīm* (< Aram. *qaddīšīn*, cf. *Ba*). Observe also that Bb is a vision with translocation, Ba is a dream; Bb ends with an admonition to keep it a secret (8:26b), Ba does not.

27b See Addendum 2, p. 62.

28 G. Dalman, *Die Worte Jesu*, p. 11 in both 1st and 2nd ed.

29 With the exception of the interpolated prayer 9:4b–20, the Hebrew of which is original.

NOTES TO SECTION V

1 That it is an interpolation was demonstrated by A. von Gall, *Die einheitlichkeit des buches Daniel*, 1895, pp. 123–6, and is almost universally recognized; the case is cogently stated in English by Charles 226 f.

2 But Charles has some good suggestions. — As can be seen from *The Journal of the American Oriental Society* 58 (1938): 540, I had been working along lines similar to those of Zimmermann at about the same time as he, tho I have only now got around to publishing on the subject. Of course I mention this only by way of emphasizing my agreement with Zimmermann, not of claiming any of the credit that is his.

3 Baumgartner *DF*, 79 n. 1.

4 Zimmermann 1938: 265; but the word hardly means 'countenance.'

5 Ibid. 266.

6 Ibid. 266.

7 Ibid. 261 f.

8 Zimmermann doesn't actually say that, as he apparently thinks that both *zky* and *dky* can have either the sense of 'to be right(eous), victorious' or that of 'to be pure, (ritually) clean.' But only *zky* can have the first meaning, and only

dky the second. — With regard to *maṣdīqe hārabbīm* (12:3), on the other hand, I agree with Zimmermann 1939: 351 that it is translated from Aramaic; but only because I regard it as established on other grounds that all the Hebrew in Daniel (except 9:4–20) is translated from Aramaic, not because *maṣdīqē harabbīm* is bad Hebrew. As a matter of fact it is very good *biblical* Hebrew; cf. Isa 53:11 (where omit *ṣaddīq* as a dittography).

[9] Both forms may be spelled *wydky*; but for *wyiḏkē*, *wydk'* is more probable in Daniel.

[10] Probably not (with Zimmermann) מהעדה, which is not a likely spelling for the *passive* participle (<**mha'dai*) which the circumstances require. — As a result of the crippling blow dealt to Antiochus III by Rome, the former's successor Seleucus IV (187–176) inherited an empire from which the territories north of the Taurus had been torn away and which staggered under the burden of an enormous war indemnity. So far, therefore, from stripping others of 'dominion, glory, and sovereignty' he was deficient in them himself. (As for the conventional exegesis, it would only be plausible if we were dealing not with translation Hebrew but with emendation Hebrew — the kind that exists only in some of the more ligneous 'restorations' of Duhm, Sellin et al.)

[11] Because this word does mean (but not here) 'potentate' as well as 'power,' Syr (perhaps aided by a recollection of 7:14) happens to have hit just on the word of which our *nōḡēś* is a mistranslation.

[12] So rightly Zimmermann 1938: 265 f.

[13] A better Hebrew rendering could have been obtained with the help of a post-biblical construction: חסוך (נטול) שלטון והדר ומלכות.

[14] Zimmermann 1938: 259 f.

[14a] In contrast to most of the heathen rulers from Cyrus to Antiochus III. On the latter see Bickerman *GM*, 51, 176–7; A. Alt *ZAW* 57 (1939): 283–5.

[See now further Bikerman, *Syria* 25 (1946–8): 67–85; cf. especially p. 83, ll. 14 ff.]

[15] G. F. Moore, *Journal of biblical literature* 15 (1896): 194, which see.

[15a] See further on.

[15b] The idea that the appalling abomination is stationed on the 'stand' (*kan* or *māḵōn*) of God or of his cult recurs in 9:27, where read כַּנָּם 'their stand' (meaning that of the banished sacrifice and offering); and it recurs again in 8:11–12, which will be expounded further on. It is also implicit in 11:31 and 12:11; cf. 1 Macc 1:54, quoted immediately ahead. — All of which, by the way, disposes of Zimmermann 1938: 264 f.; but also of those who read כנו 'its stand' (a graphically improbable emendation of the masoretic כנף) in 9:27, which would imply that God's altar was the proper stand of the appalling abomination! It further disposes of Torrey *JBL* 66 (1947): 268–272; for it renders it more impossible than ever to make 9:27b refer to anything but the semi-septennium beginning late in 167, or v. 27 as a whole to anything but the complete septennium beginning some time in 170, and consequently v. 26a to anything but the murder of the high priest Onias III in 170 B.C.E.

[16] See Bickerman *GM*, 92-6, 111–6.

[17] Zimmermann 1938: 257–9 rightly attributes the frequently puzzling presence or absence of the article in the Hebrew of Daniel to its character as a translation

from Aramaic. But I would correct him as follows. The translator erred, not because his original did not distinguish sharply between determinate and indeterminate (tho the Aramaic portions of Daniel might make such an impression upon one who expected every language with the means of making such distinctions to apply them according to exactly the same rules as English, a misconception against which see B.-L. para. 88) but because it did so by subtle inflection where the Hebrew did it by the use or non-use of a distinct lexical element. Having picked up his languages by reading and speaking them, but never having been drilled in the rendering of Hebrew nomina with and without articles into Aramaic or of Aramaic nomina in the absolute and emphatic states into Hebrew, he probably employed them all correctly in free composition but naturally made slips in translation.

[18] Cf. Lev 11:43, 44b; 20:25.

[19] Of the Seleucid era Jewish style = Nisan 167 thru Addar 166.

[19a] See E. Schürer, *Geschichte des jüdischen volkes im zeitalter Jesu Christi*[3] II, 1898: 559–60. — I owe this observation to Prof. Lieberman.

[20] The text and purport of this verse have been discussed on p. 34.

[21] As is well known the ktib in Daniel preserves the original form of the emphatic nisbeh *-āyā*, which the qre changes to *-ā'ā*.

[22] Cf. n. 20. — It may be recalled that the name גבריאל is first introduced at a spot (8:16) which suggests that its bearer is so named because he looks like a גבר (8:15).

[23] Otiose ה after ו is sufficiently frequent to raise the question whether it is not a vowel-letter like the ה after ש in שה־שמם (var. ש־שמם), Lam 5:18; שה־תקיף (var. ש־תקיף), Koh 6:10; שה־שאול (var. ש-שאול), Mishnah Abot 4:22; or like the ה after כ in כה־חכם, Koh 8:1. Cf. וה־מדינות, Koh 2:8; וה־סכלות, 7:25; also ־ואי in the Hadad inscription; see *Journal of the American Oriental Society* 62 (1942): 235–6. — וה־פשע, Dan 8:13, may come under this heading.

[24] Zimmermann 1939: 350 has already called attention to the translator's similar mechanical rendering of *šabbū'īn* by *šābū'īm* instead of *šābū'ōt*. (9:24, 25, 26; 10:2).

[25] See above, n. 17.

[26] See above, p. 43.

[27] So still Bentzen.

[28] See above, n. 15b.

[29] In v. 5 Zimmermann 1938: 208 f. seems to me to be on the right track when he traces חזות to an Aramaic חֲזְיָה, which means literally 'seen.' But the sense he is content to extract from the recovered Aramaic phrase קרן חזיה בין עינוהי, namely 'a horn was seen on its forehead,' is much too insipid for 'the big horn' of vv. 8, 21. As for our verse (v. 8), his reconstruction of its Aramaic original involves the improbable assumption that the translator was acquainted with the feminine plural perfect form *qṭálā*, which is Babylonian and targumic (see above Section I B 2). I therefore suggest that the recovered passive participle feminine *ḥazyā* in v. 5 be assigned the gerundive sense of 'visible,' i. e. 'stout' (cf. on 7:20, above Section II n. 47a and the text preceding that note) and the whole phrase translated 'there was a stout horn on its forehead'; and that in v. 8 חזות be pre-

sumed to represent the plural of *ḥazyā* namely *ḥazyān* (חֶזְיָן) 'visible ones,' that is to say 'stout ones.' With the stout horn of v. 5 and the four stout ones of v. 8 is contrasted the 'little' horn of v. 9.

30 Many mss., 2 edd.: מהן; Baumgartner *BHK*3 ad loc.

31 Sebirin, a few mss., 1 ed.: יצאה; ibid.

32 Did the translator have in mind a feminine of the properly indeclinable (because substantival) מִצְעָר of Gen 19:20, because he felt that צעיר properly means 'younger' or 'youngest' (son, daughter, clan)? See the lexica on צעיר.

33 Perhaps על: 'it magnified itself *over* the Prince of the host'; Baumgartner, ibid.

34 Cf. Baumgartner *BHK*3 ad loc.

35 Perhaps vocalize *wā-pešā'*; cf. above, n. 23.

36 Perhaps an intrusion from 9:27; 11:31; 12:11.

37 So rightly Baumgartner *BHK*,3 with LXX, Th, Syr.

38 'His' is in any case better English than 'the'; and perhaps the original Aramaic actually had *qrnh*, which was intended to represent *qarneh* 'his horn' but was read *qarnā* 'the horn' by the translator.

39 I. e. Palestine; cf. 11:16, 41, 45; after Jer 3:19; Ezek 20:6, 15. — In our passage, however, the word is probably an exuberance; see Montgomery, philological note.

40 Possibly 'sanctity,' i. e. all that is sacred. However, 'sanctuary' is the more natural meaning of *miqdāš* (so here and 11:31; as against *qoḏeš*, which has more often the general meaning of 'holiness').

41 See above, nn. 23, 35.

42 I. e. until an aggregate of 2300 daily evening and morning sacrifices have been omitted, i. e. until 1150 days have elapsed.

43 See the introductory paragraph of this Section. LXX and Th, guided by the context also render *καθαρισθήσεται*.

44 See above, n. 15.

45 See above, p. 48 f.

45a See below C 13.

46 See Syr and Section I B 2.

47 See above, n. 29.

48 Perhaps better יעת. יעא means specifically 'to sprout' and is yet etymologically identical with the more general יצא of the Hebrew text.

49 חדה corresponds exactly to the Hebrew, and is more suitable here than אחרי, which is appropriate in 7:8 because the eleventh horn there is of the same order as the preceding ten (=kings).

50 See above, n. 33.

51 Syr renders both *māḵōn* in 8:11b and *kann-* in 11:20, 38 by *matqan*.

52 The uncontracted haphel imperfect is the rule in Daniel, and תהפס was more likely than תפס to be mistaken for תרפס. But under the influence of the preceding occurrences of רפס it could have happened with תפס too.

53 If this word rather than קשט represents the original of the Hebrew אמת, there may be here an allusion to the Aramaic proverb יציבא בארעא וגיורא בשמי שמיא 'The native below and the stranger above!' (TP Ḥagigah 76a; TB Erubin 9a; Baba

Qama 42a; Yoma 47a); than which, it will be agreed, none could be more apropos. In fact, I wonder if the original of פשע was not גּוֹר 'adultery' (Syr *gaurā*); which, in spite of its specialized signification, the author may have chosen for the sake of its resemblance to גִּיוֹר.

54 In this way, perhaps, the strange לפלמוני of the Hebrew may be accounted for.

55 This word may be omitted if we assume that the Aramaic of this author employed the *dual* of אלף.

56 We know this word very well from A 1. קדישין, the term used in ch. 7, could not have been confounded with חיל any more than with חסן.

57 Perhaps the verb *(h)appes* 'to profane' followed by an expression synonymous with *ḥsain* 'saints' figured in still a third passage and has there been rendered in still a third manner. In the clause וככלות נַפֵּץ יד עם קדש, Dan 12:7b, Bevan, taking a hint from the LXX (which, however, probably did not itself have before it a reading different from ours), transposes the second and third words, vocalizes the first one *wḵiḵlōṯ*, and further vocalizes נפץ as the participle *nōpēṣ*, which would be a unique occurrence of the qal of this verb; while Charles (p. 335 n. 1) emends this word to *nōṯēṣ* 'one who pulls down (a structure)' — which (even for our translator) is too unidiomatic in the context to be worth the considerable alteration of the graphic picture which it involves — or (comparing Jer 51:20–24; also 50:23) to *mappēṣ* 'battle-ax,' of which one can't very well say 'when its hand, or strength, fails.' Moreover, with or without any of these emendations, the verse speaks of the 'shattering' or 'shatterer' of the Jews; and that, especially in the light of the Jeremiah passages, suggests military conquest rather than religious persecution. Antiochus IV, however, did not subjugate the Jews, who had been subject to his two predecessors before him; and even Antiochus III had defeated not the Jews but a rival Macedonian (Ptolemy V) to whom the Jews had been subject. In any case, the military and political aspects of Antiochus IV's relations with the Jews were completely overshadowed by the religious. It is not for nothing that the Jews in relation to Antiochus IV are consistently referred to as 'pious ones' or 'holy ones' (see above, e. g. n. 56, and further on); and our passage, in which they are called עַם קֹדֶשׁ 'holy people,' is no exception.

Let us therefore formulate the problem of נַפֵּץ as follows: what Aramaic verb is employed elsewhere in connection with Antiochus's oppression of 'saints'? The (h)aphel of *pss*, of course. The participle of this would be *mhappes* or the later, contracted, form *mappes*. [(H)aphel participles are mostly contracted in Daniel; e. g. 5:19b.] But the consonants of the latter can also be read *mippas*; which is the qal infinitive, or verbal noun, of the same root and means 'dividing, taking apart,' and in Palestinian Aramaic probably even 'breaking up' since *pss* has this sense in tannaitic Hebrew; see S. Lieberman, *Tosefet Rishonim* IV, p. 64 *ad* ll. 32/33. And this interpretation was all the likelier to occur to the translator because one does not commonly talk of profaning people alone (in the Daniel and Maccabees passages dealt with in the text the phrase is 'to profane sanctuary and saints'). Accordingly, while tentatively accepting the change of word order and the interpretation of וככלות upon which the rendering of the Septuagint is predicated, I reject the further emendations of both Bevan and Charles. וככלות

יד נַפֵּץ עם קדש means 'and when the strength of the breaking up of a holy people shall fail.' That is harsh, but only because נפץ 'breaking up' is a mistranslation of מפס, as just explained. Substitute מחלל 'desecrater,' and all is well.

[In the light of what we have made out about the Aramaic substratum of 8:11, 13; (11:31) 12:7, Zimmermann 1938: 260–1 — improbable on other grounds — is questionable also because it posits the use of *'a(ḥ)ḥel* (instead of *'appes*) 'to profane' in the Aramaic original.]

58 If the terrifying figure had only appeared to Daniel in a vision (1) it could not have been prevented from doing so for twenty-one days by its engagement with the prince of Persia (10:12–13), and (2) Daniel's companions could not have sensed its presence despite their inability to see it (10:7).

58a See above, IV B, especially p. 76, n. 11.

59 That the LXX's Hebrew manuscript had אחוית, as Charles supposes, is exceedingly improbable.

60 Since *'aḥwāyā* rendered *'aḥrīṯ* in 12:8 and *'aḥwāyā* rendered *mar'ē* in 8:16, 26a, 27b are from the hand of the author of ch. 9 (see Section IV), does the same apply to the remaining example of *'aḥwāyā* rendered *mar'ē*, in 10:1bβ? It is at any rate a fact that in 9:23 'so consider the word and attend to the oracle (or interpretation)' follows very naturally on what precedes, while in 10:1 'and he considered (?) the word and attended to (?) the oracle (or interpretation)' is very superfluous.

61 Of course isolated third feminine plural forms with *y* preformative occur in early Hebrew literature (Gen 30:38; 1 Sam 6:12); but if they were what the writer had in mind he would not have used the *y* performative and the *t* preformative with the same verb in one sentence, and with the *y* preformative just in the case where the Aramaic would have used the imperfect and the *t* where it would not have.

62 See Section I B 2, and cf. Syr. — Logically we should have had here *usliqī*, Heb. *watta'lēnā*, cf. v. 8; but the interpretation has influenced the recapitulation of the vision.

63 On 11:15, 22, 31, see above p. 48.

64 See Section IV, n. 16.

64a Possibly the author of the secondary verse 8:16 (see Section IV B) was not clear in his mind either about just what sort of a thing the א[ו]בל אולי of v. 2 was, but the author of the original apocalypse Bb (ch. 8 minus later expansions — See Section IV B) certainly meant the Ulai Gate. The only serious objection to this interpretation that Waterman, *JBL* 66 (1947): 319–20, has raised is in the last paragraph of that note. It does not in any case balance the arguments on the other side, and even it is at least partly canceled by the circumstance that in Aramaic, if not in Accadian, a city can have more than one *ᵃḇol*, TB Erubin 6b; Yoma 11a; Targum to Jer 50:26 (with which cf., with the lexica of Levy and Jastrow under אבולא, the corresponding word in the Peshitta). [I see now from Delitzsch, *Assyr. Hwb.*, 7a, that a town can have more than one *abullu* in Accadian too.]

65 See above, sub-Section A 2.

[66] See above, n. 17, on the precise distinction between determinate and indeterminate in the Aramaic of Daniel (and in Palestinian Aramiaic generally). The exact phrase אנחנה . . . משח לא משח(י)ן וחמר לא שתין occurs in Cowley, *Aramaic Papyri of the Fifth Century*, 30:20 and 31:19–20.

[67] See above, para. 1.

[68] Compare the conclusion: but it shall fail. See above, para. 3.

INDEX OF PASSAGES

Genesis

7:11 70
8: 2 70
14: 1 73
19:1 59
19:20 82
30:38 84
42:19, 33 3
49:25 70

Exodus

20: 4 70

Leviticus

1:17 69
11:43 81
11:44 81
20:25 81

Numbers

24:24 78
25 49

Deuteronomy

5: 8 70
10:17 8
26: 8 48
28:40 60
33:13 70

Judges

7:16 61
9:43 61
14:18 13
19:30 59

I Samuel

2:30 49
6:12 84

II Samuel

1:23 13
17: 8 13

I Kings

14: 9 56

II Kings

19:22 68
20:11 73
20:12 73
25:27 19
25:27–30 25

Isaiah

7: 7 57
8: 8 .... 49, 78
10 37
10: 5–6 64
10: 5 78
10:15 78
10:23–26 78
13: 3 15
13:17 15
13:17–19 15
21: 2 15
30:15–16 64
37:23 68
38: 8 73
39: 1 73
41: 4 70
43:10 70
48: 3 70
51:10 70
53:11 80

Jeremiah

3:19 82
4—6 14

5:15–17 14
6: 4 78
10:11 65
25:34 2
27: 5 ff. 64
50:23 83
50:26 84
50:28 15
51:11 15
51:20–24 83
51:28 15
52:31 19
52:31–34 25

Ezekiel

12:27 78
16: 9 60
20: 6, 15 82
21:36 78

Hosea

13: 8 13

Amos

6: 6 60
7: 4 70

Micah

6:15 60

Habakkuk

1: 6, 14 ff. 14
2: 2–3 .... 34, 35
2: 3 .... 35, 36, 37
2: 5 14

Psalms

10: 5 78
12: 6 78
27:12 78
31: 3 46
36: 7 70
79 28
90: 1–2 70
90:10 77
137:8–9 15

Proverbs

6:19 78
12:17 78
14: 5 78
17:12 13
19: 5 78
19: 9 78
26: 3 56

Job

18:17 65

Canticles

2:17 78
4: 6 78
4:16 78

Lamentations

5:18 81

Koheleth

2: 8 81
2:18–19 75
6:10 81
7:25 81
8: 1 81
12: 3 69

Esther

1 73
1: 1 72
1: 3 73
1: 3–8 75
1:14 73
1:18 73
1:19 73
10 73
10: 2 73

Ezra

4:23 . . . 48
6:14 . . . 72

Nehemiah

1: 1 . . . 70
2: 4 . . . 45
12:22 . . . 19

Daniel

1 . . . 64
1—6 . . . 9, 27, 64, 68
1: 1—2:4a . . . 38, 39, 41, 76
1:15 . . . 39
1:17 . . . 39
1:18 . . . 39
2 . . . 5 ff., 26, 27, 29, 37, 64, 65, 67, 68
2: 1 . . . 59, 64
2: 4b—6:29 . . . 38, 65
2:10 . . . 58
2:16 . . . 50
2:17–23 . . . 27
2:23 . . . 43
2:27–28 . . . 27
2:28 . . . 55
2:31 . . . 68, 71
2:33 . . . 67
2:34 . . . 71
2:34–35 . . . 6, 65, 66
2:35 . . . 6, 71
2:37 . . . 46
2:37–38 . . . 25, 66
2:37–39 . . . 13, 26
2:38 . . . 26, 64
2:39 . . . 26, 65, 77
2:39–40 . . . 11
2:40 . . . 59, 65
2:40–41 . . . 67
2:41 . . . 42, 61, 65, 66, 67
2:41–43 . . . 8
2:42 . . . 65
2:43 . . . 42, 58
2:44 . . . 6, 65, 66
2:47 . . . 1, 8, 27
3 . . . 28
3: 5 . . . 59
3: 8 . . . 28
3:12 . . . 28, 58
3:13 . . . 2
3:14 . . . 58
3:16 . . . 58
3:23 . . . 39
3:24 . . . 59
4 . . . 28, 64
4: 2 . . . 50
4: 4 . . . 58
4: 6 . . . 58
4: 7 . . . 68
4: 8 . . . 71
4:10 . . . 3, 68
4:13 . . . 1
4:17 . . . 71
4:19 . . . 25
4:20 . . . 1
4:22 . . . 1
4:26 . . . 39
4:29 . . . 1
4:31 . . . 50
4:33 . . . 2, 50
5 . . . 11, 27, 28, 29, 64, 75
5: 5 . . . 4
5: 8 . . . 58
5: 9 . . . 41
5:12 . . . 55
5:13 . . . 2
5:15 . . . 2
5:18–19 . . . 25
5:19 . . . 83
5:20 . . . 63
5:23 . . . 58
5:24–27 . . . 75
5:25 . . . 24, 75
5:26–27 . . . 24, 25, 26
5:27 . . . 41
5:29 . . . 60
6 . . . 27, 73, 77
6: 1 . . . 13, 77
6: 7 . . . 60
6:12 . . . 60
6:15–29 . . . 67

6:16 . . . 60
6:17 . . . 48
6:18 . . . 2
6:21 . . . 48
6:24 . . . 2
7 . . . 5 ff., 22, 26, 29, 31, 32, 34, 38, 39, 46, 64, 67, 68, 70, 72, 74, 75, 83
7—12 . . . 19, 27, 64
7: 1–7 . . . 15
7: 2 . . . 3, 11
7: 3 . . . 3, 15, 70 n. 36
7: 4 . . . 2, 10, 11, 12, 14, 63, 65, 68, 69, 71, 72
7: 4–5 . . . 10, 15, 69, 72
7: 4–7 . . . 63
7: 5 . . . 2, 3, 11, 12, 13, 14, 63, 69, 72
7: 5 f. . . . 77
7: 6 . . . 3, 11, 12
7: 7 . . . 3, 10, 11 ff., 21, 54, 69, 74
7: 8 . . . 3, 4, 11, 30, 65, 71, 74, 75, 82
7: 8–28 . . . 16–18
7: 9 . . . 71
7: 9 ff. . . . 65
7: 9–10 . . . 10
7:10 . . . 48
7:11 . . . 2, 10, 65, 71
7:11–12 . . . 67
7:12 . . . 6, 10, 22, 63, 65, 66
7:13 . . . 7, 11, 68, 70
7:14 . . . 80
7:16 . . . 50
7:17 . . . 65, 74
7:18 . . . 6, 7, 68
7:19 . . . 21, 54, 69
7:20 . . . 4, 11 ff., 21, 30, 70, 71, 81
7:21 . . . 7
7:21 f. . . . 30, 68
7:22 . . . 7
7:23 . . . 21, 65
7:23–27 . . . 71
7:24 11 ff., 18, 21, 22, 62, 65, 70, 71, 74
7:24–25 . . . 71
7:25 . . . 1, 7, 30, 33, 61, 68
7:27 . . . 6, 7, 68
7:28 . . . 33, 41, 50, 59
8 . . . 20, 22, 23, 29, 30, 31, 33, 34, 36, 42, 48, 49 ff., 64, 68, 70, 79, 84
8—12 . . 21, 29 f., 38, 39, 41, 59, 74, 76
8: 1 . . . 32, 34, 36
8: 2 . . . 32, 57, 70, 84
8: 2–12 . . . 32
8: 3 . . . 30, 57, 73
8: 3 f. . . . 77
8: 4 . . . 56
8: 5 . . . 30, 57, 58, 70, 81, 82
8: 6 . . . 57
8: 7 . . . 52, 53
8: 7–14 . . . 51–52
8: 7–14 . . . 53–54
8: 8 . . . 30, 70, 81–82, 84
8: 9 . . . 8, 30, 49, 71, 82
8: 9–10 . . . 50
8: 9–12 . . . 70, 78
8: 9–14 . . . 20
8:10 . . . 52, 53
8:10–11 . . . 53
8:10–12 . . . 44
8:10–13 . . . 52
8:11 . . . 49, 50, 51, 53, 82 n. 40, 84
8:11–12 . . . 30, 49, 50, 80
8:11b–12 . . . 51, 54
8:11–13 . . . 53
8:12 . . . 32, 49, 50, 51, 60
8:13 . . . 32, 49, 50, 51, 54, 81, 84
8:13–14 . . . 32, 37, 76
8:14 . . . 33, 41, 77
8:15 . . . 32, 76, 81
8:15–25 . . . 32
8:16 . . . 32, 33, 37, 55, 79, 81, 84
8:17 . . . 32, 33, 35, 36, 37, 59, 76, 79
8:18 . . . 36, 37, 59
8:18–19 . . . 32, 36, 37, 59
8:19 . . . 35, 36, 37, 79
8:20 . . . 77
8:20–21 . . . 56
8:21 . . . 70, 77, 81
8:21–22 . . . 77
8:21–23 . . . 68
8:22 . . . 42, 48, 56, 61, 77

8:23–24 ... 20
8:23–25 ... 78
8:24 ... 30, 32, 46, 79
8:24–25 ... 30
8:25 ... 32, 53
8:26 ... 32, 33, 35, 36, 37, 55, 58, 76, 78, 79, 84
8:27 ... 32, 33, 37, 55, 56, 57, 58, 84
9 ... 23, 29, 33, 34, 37, 64, 79, 84
9: 1 ... 13, 34, 59, 72, 77
9: 2–3 ... 79
9: 4–20 ... 33, 38, 41, 50, 79, 80
9:21 ... 33, 34, 79
9:23 ... 55, 79, 84
9:24 ... 33, 57, 79, 81
9:25 ... 81
9:26 ... 80, 81
9:27 ... 30, 33, 45, 77, 80, 82
10 ... 37
10—12 ... 19, 23, 29, 30, 34, 59, 64, 79
10: 1 ... 19, 55, 77, 84
10: 2 ... 31, 81
10: 2–3 ... 30, 36
10: 3 ... 34, 60
10 :4 ... 36
10 :6 ... 55
10: 7 ... 55, 84
10: 8 ... 41, 55
10: 9 ... 37, 59
10:12 ... 30, 31
10:12–13 ... 84
10:12–14 ... 34
10:13 ... 60
10:14 ... 35, 78, 79
10:16 ... 55
10:18 ... 46
10:19 ... 30, 31
10:20 ... 47, 60
10:20–21 ... 34
10:20—11:2 ... 34
10:21 ... 30, 31, 34, 36
11 ... 42 ff., 53, 54, 74
11: 1 ... 34, 42, 46
11: 2 ... 19
11: 2 ff. ... 34
11: 4 ... 61
11: 6 ... 47, 48
11: 7 ... 42, 46, 47, 49
11: 8 ... 47
11: 9 ... 47
11:10 ... 42, 47, 49, 78
11:11 ... 30
11:12 ... 48
11:14 ... 79
11:15 ... 48, 84
11:16 ... 8, 82
11:17 ... 57, 61
11:19 ... 42, 48
11:20 ... 42, 82
11:22 ... 48, 78, 84
11:23 ... 41
11:26 ... 78
11:27 ... 35, 37, 61
11:28 ... 49
11:29 ... 1
11:29–39 ... 42
11:30 ... 49, 78
11:31 ... 42, 45, 46, 48, 50, 53, 54, 80, 82, 84
11:31 ff. ... 30
11:33 ... 41
11:35 ... 35, 37, 41
11:36 ... 30, 44, 53, 78
11:36–8 ... 44
11:37 ... 43, 44, 53
11:38 ... 42, 43, 44, 46, 49, 53, 82
11:39 ... 42, 43, 46, 49, 53, 61
11:40 ... 49, 78
11:40 ff. ... 62
11:41 ... 8, 82
11:45 ... 82
12 ... 31, 33
12: 1 ... 59
12: 3 ... 80
12: 4 ... 30, 31, 32, 33, 36, 76
12: 5–10 ... 31, 34
12: 6 ... 34
12: 7 ... 1, 30, 33, 34, 46, 61, 76, 83, 84
12: 8 ... 55, 58, 84
12:11 ... 37, 38, 45,48, 50, 76, 80, 82
12:11–12 ... 38

12:12 . . . . . 37, 38, 76, 77
12:13 . . . . . 31, 34

I Maccabees

1 54
1: 1 78
1:10–40 74
1:33 43
1:44–54 . . . . . 45–46, 54
1:46 . . . . . 46, 48
1:54 . . . . . 46, 48, 51, 76, 77, 80
3:36, 45 43
4:52–53 76
8: 5 78

Jubilees

46: 6 78

Mishnah

Abot 2, 3, 4 65
Abot 4:22 81
Nega'im 1:1 71

Tosefta

Rosh ha-shanah p. 211, 1. 10 76

Talmud Palaestinense

Rosh ha-shanah II 58b 71
Ḥagigah 76a 82

Talmud Babylonicum

Shabbat 54a 71
'Erubin 6b 84
'Erubin 9a 82
Yoma 11a 84
Yoma 47a 82
Rosh ha-shanah 3b 72
Megillah 12a 73
Baba Qamma 42a 82
Sanhedrin 108a 71

Midrashim

Seder 'olam rabbah 28 73
Seder 'olam rabbah 29, 30 (p. 136 f.) 72
Seder 'olam zuṭṭa 19
Genesis rabbah 26:6 71
Canticles rabbah 3:3 73
Esther rabbah 3 73
Esther rabbah to 1:4 75
Midrash Abba Gorion to Esth 1:4. 75

Targums

See above Gen 42:19, 33; Lev 1:17; Num 24:24; 25; Deut 26:8; Jer 50:26; Ps 31:3; Esther 1:1

Jewish papyri 85

Christian Sources

Revelation 14:8 69
Lactantius *Div. inst.* VII, 15:11, 19. 65
Jerome on Dan 7:8 75

Pagan Sources

Ahikar papyri, 1. 67 39
Strabo XI, 5:6; 13:1 66
Dio Cassius LXVIII 14:4 76
Porphyry *apud* Jerome 75

www.ingramcontent.com/pod-product-compliance
Ingram Content Group UK Ltd.
Pitfield, Milton Keynes, MK11 3LW, UK
UKHW021304180426
11947UKWH00015B/1000

9 780873 341073